Recode Your Life: From Chaos to Clarity

Anna Izmirian

Disclaimer: This book is a collection of personal thoughts, experiences, and ideas. It is not intended as professional advice in any area—financial, health, legal, or otherwise. This book is not a substitute for professional medical advice, diagnosis, or treatment. While it encourages self-awareness and a proactive approach to health, it is essential to consult qualified healthcare professionals for medical concerns, diagnoses, and treatment plans. Always seek the advice of a doctor or other licensed health provider before making any changes to your health regimen.

The author has made every effort to ensure accuracy but assumes no responsibility for errors or omissions. Any perceived slights against organizations or individuals are unintentional.

The opinions expressed are solely those of the author and do not reflect the views or policies of any financial institution, regulatory body, or employer.

This book does not constitute an offer or solicitation to buy or sell any financial products, securities, or investments. The strategies and principles discussed are intended to promote general financial literacy, productivity, and personal development.

The author and publisher assume no responsibility for any errors or omissions or for any outcomes resulting from the application of the information provided. By reading this book, you acknowledge that you are solely responsible for your own financial and personal decisions.

Table of Contents

- Love, Intimacy, & Partnership
- Family & Raising Children
- Healthy Friendships

6. Mastering Time & Energy

- The Illusion of Time
- Automation vs. Presence

7. Learning & Career Growth

5

A smart Person

A smart person is not the one who holds endless facts in their mind,

not the one who recites knowledge like a well-trained parrot,

not the one who drowns in books yet remains blind to life itself.

A truly wise soul is one who **sees, who listens, who understands**—

one who does not merely collect information, but weaves it into meaning,

one who does not simply remember, but knows when and how to apply.

Such a person moves through life with measured steps,

tracing the unseen lines that connect cause and effect,

seeing the path from A to B before the journey has even begun.

They do not mistake their own intelligence for its limit,

for they know the mind is a vast and boundless field,

a river that deepens, a sky that stretches farther with every step.

To be truly wise is to remain forever a student,

to expand, to absorb, to master, yet never to claim mastery.

A smart person is **patient**, for they know time bends to those who wait.

A smart person is **loving**, for they understand the weight of a kind word.

A smart person is **humble**, for arrogance is the death of wisdom.

They are both **dreamer and realist**, both **firm and yielding**,

seeing life as it is, yet never fearing to shape it into something more.

For the mind is not a vessel to be filled,

but a **fire to be kindled**—

and those who tend to it with care shall never cease to burn.

Introduction

Why I Wrote This Book

If life were a city—let's take Vienna, one of my favourite places—then the search for truth would be like meeting at Stephansplatz. No matter where you start, if you're truly searching for it, you'll find yourself arriving there eventually. Some may take the scenic route, some may get lost and double back, while others may find shortcuts along the way. But regardless of the roads taken, the destination remains the same. Like life, we follow different clues, experiences, and detours, only to realize that despite our unique paths, we all seek the same core truths—happiness, health, fulfillment, and purpose.

I am not building new roads to get to Stephanplatz. In fact, no one writing any book is truly building new roads—we all have the map. It was programmed into our DNA, written about since the beginning of time. The wisdom has always been there, but over generations, we've forgotten it. Every so often, someone rediscovers the path and wants to share a simpler way to reach the destination. My goal is not to reinvent the journey but to help clear the unnecessary detours, making the road easier to navigate.

Some ideas in this book may not be new or groundbreaking—perhaps you've heard variations of them before. But maybe some are fresh, or at least presented in a way that finally resonates.

At the end of the day, the task remains the same—to make life better. While we are all unique in our circumstances, upbringing, culture, health, and appearance, at our core, we seek the same things: happiness, love, purpose, and fulfillment. No matter the path we take or the obstacles we face, the search is universal. Everyone, in their own way, is navigating toward the same truths.

And let's be honest—before you even start reading my book wouldn't you want to know

"Who is this person? What makes her qualified to give me advice?"

I could talk about my hardships and tell you why they make me uniquely qualified to give advice, but the truth is—hardship is relative. What may seem like a great struggle to one person might be just another challenge to someone else. Our experiences shape us, but they are not etched into our core—our core remains pure. We are not bound by our past, nor are we limited by the circumstances that once defined us. What truly matters is how we interpret, grow from, and apply those lessons. The power lies in our ability to continuously evolve, to shed what no longer serves us, and to refine our perspective in pursuit of a more fulfilling life.

I won't go into too much detail about my personal life—both to protect my privacy and to respect those closest to me. But I will say this: At this point, I've lived about half a century. Naturally, when I look back, I acknowledge that I've learned a great deal. Compared to some, I've achieved a lot in life; compared to others, I may be far behind, but success is relative, and **the value of a life isn't measured in comparisons—it's measured in experiences, growth, and the impact of our thoughts.** Many of history's greatest writers—Dante, Shakespeare, Socrates—were, in their own times, just ordinary people. Yet centuries later, their words remain alive, shaping the minds of those who come after them. Writing, at its core, is about sharing experiences, perspectives, and ideas in the hope that they resonate with someone. Whether this book finds success or never sells a single copy, the process of writing it has been deeply inspiring for me. It's a reflection of everything I've learned, unlearned, and come to understand about life. If my words help even one person think differently, move forward, or find clarity, then that is success enough. As you read my book, keep in mind that much of what I share comes from personal experience — often from doing the exact opposite and learning the hard way. My mistakes have been my greatest teachers, and it's through those lessons that I've gained the insights I'm now passing on to you.

My perspective is shaped by a life lived in extremes. In just one lifetime —I've experienced both privilege and struggle, stability and upheaval. I was born into a wealthy family, where a chauffeur drove me to school, but when that luxury was gone, it was replaced with something far more valuable—an intellectual environment that prioritized nature, good food, health, and the ability to build something from nothing.

I have lived through profound loss—losing a parent, witnessing cities reduced to rubble by earthquakes, surviving war and hunger. They say, "What doesn't kill you makes you stronger." And in many ways, that's true, but the greatest challenge wasn't enduring those moments—it was learning to navigate a world consumed by materialism and relentless societal expectations. True resilience isn't just about surviving disaster; it's about resisting the distractions that pull you away from what truly matters.

A new life in a new country brought fresh challenges—marriage, raising a family, and the constant balancing act of building a future within capitalism. I've seen my family create wealth and lose it more than once, but real hardship doesn't come from financial loss. The two forces that truly break people? **Health and consumerism.** One limits your ability to live, the other convinces you that no matter how much you have, it will never be enough.

Experience Over Theory

In Judaism, unlike many other religions, a rabbi must be married and have children. **Why?**

Because when he preaches to his community, his words must come from lived experience—not theory. If he's talking about marriage, about raising children, about handling family struggles, he must have lived it himself. Otherwise, his words are just empty ideals.

The same applies to this book.

I'm not writing from a detached, theoretical perspective. I'm writing as someone who has been thrown curveballs in life, someone who has fallen and gotten back up, someone who is still analyzing, still learning, still striving to live the best life possible.

Before we dive into the details, let's establish a foundation—a simple framework I call *The Pillars of Life: A Framework for Lasting Change.* **Just as a strong building needs solid pillars, a fulfilling life is built on a few essential areas: health, relationships, financial stability, personal growth, purpose, time management, and environment.** Neglect one, and the others suffer. Strengthen them, and everything falls into place. As you read this book, think about which areas need the most attention in your life and how you can begin making small, meaningful shifts.

The most crucial takeaway from this book is going to be an absolute self-respect. At the end of the day, you should be able to look back at your life and know, without a doubt, that you gave your best in every situation.

That inner voice—the one that tells you to stop smoking, to read a book, to work out—needs to carry weight. It needs to hold authority over your actions, not be dismissed or drowned out by excuses. The stronger your self-respect, the more you'll trust that voice and when you listen to it, you'll realize that self-discipline isn't about restriction—it's about building a life you're proud of.

You need to be proud of your actions—proud of the choices you make every single day. That pride builds self-respect, and self-respect, in turn, strengthens the authority of your inner voice.

When you consistently act in alignment with your values, that voice no longer feels like a nagging thought or a fleeting moment of motivation—it becomes a true command center, one that you trust and obey without hesitation. The more you reinforce this internal authority, the easier it becomes to follow through on your goals, make disciplined decisions, and ultimately shape the life you want.

Let's get started.

The Simplicity That Saves Us

Most people live to possess, not to evolve—trading the essence of life for the illusion of ownership. (Anna I)

Some may dismiss my words as idealistic.

Some may say simplicity is naïve, but here's what I know to be true:

Simplicity isn't just a lifestyle choice—it's survival.

We are drowning in noise.

Overstimulated, overburdened, overwhelmed.

The world tells us to **chase more, consume more, achieve more**—but it never teaches us how to simply **be**, and that is why so many people feel lost. This book is about reclaiming control. It's about cutting through the chaos, stripping away what doesn't matter, and finding clarity in what does.

Because if we don't, we aren't just heading toward individual burnout.

We are walking straight into **colloctive collapse**.

We live in a time of abundance—yet we are more anxious than ever.

- Information overload.
- Endless choices.
- Constant distractions.

Ironically, instead of making life easier, this excess has made us **more stressed, more dissatisfied, more disconnected from ourselves**.

We chase the next productivity hack, the latest diet, the newest investment trend— only to find ourselves trapped in the same exhausting cycle.

The truth?

Success, fulfillment, and well-being are not found in complexity. Countless books offer valuable insights into personal growth, but I found myself wishing for one that tied it all together in a simple, actionable way. That's exactly what this book does. It provides a **simple system for achieving complex things**—whether it's optimizing your health, mastering your mindset, or reaching financial freedom.

Because at the end of the day, the key to a better life isn't about adding more.

It's about **removing what's unnecessary**—until only what truly matters remains.

Our minds, when given the right circumstances — freed from jealousy, competition, and the constant noise of the world — have an extraordinary capacity to soar. Like a bird released from its cage, the subconscious can stretch its wings and tap into limitless potential. Yet, instead of nurturing this freedom, we often suppress it.

Drugs, alcohol, smoking — these are the chains we willingly place upon ourselves, numbing the very source of our power. The mind craves stimuli, growth, and liberation. It flourishes when challenged, learns when curious, and finds clarity in stillness. Without the weight of negativity and self-inflicted limitations, it can achieve boundless creativity, wisdom, and peace. We're limiting our abilities by focusing on creating an AI that will replace us mentally and physically, when we have the capacity to grow, evolve, and unlock our own untapped potential.

I have nothing against advancements in technology. In fact, I believe it's an incredible achievement — a testament to human progress and ingenuity, but the real question is, will we have the strength and discipline to use it for the greater good? Will we harness it to improve lives, heal the environment, and restore freedom? Will we continue the cycle of growth, making the world a better place? Or will we allow it to consume us, destroying what little remains of what is pure and untouched? I am a Gen-Xer, one of the last to witness both sides — a life with and without technology. Growing up in a barely-there town, I remember the simplicity of human connection, the unfiltered joys of nature, and the resilience built from solving problems without screens and instant solutions, but now, as I look around, I see a different world. The newer generations, raised in the constant hum of notifications and algorithm-fed desires, are becoming more robotic. Convenience has replaced effort. Endless stimulation has silenced curiosity. And rather than mastering technology, many are enslaved by it. Yet, I still believe we have a choice. Technology, like any tool, is neither good nor evil. Its impact depends on the hands that wield it. We can use it to free minds instead of trapping them. We can design systems that amplify human potential instead of diminishing it.

But that requires intention. Discipline. Awareness.

The world doesn't need more mindless scrolling or soulless automation. It needs creators, thinkers, and leaders willing to break the cycle — to use technology to uplift, not control.

I've seen both sides, and now, standing at the crossroads, I choose growth.

Simplicity isn't just a philosophy—it's a system. The most efficient technologies and brilliant inventions aren't complicated. They're intuitive, streamlined, and built for efficiency. The same logic applies to us.

The human mind is the most powerful operating system in existence, yet many of us never take control of how it runs.

Why can people of any age learn to use a smartphone or a computer?
Because technology mirrors the way our brains naturally function.

Now, imagine **reversing** that logic:
What if we treated our minds the same way we treat technology?
What if we believed we could reprogram our thoughts, upgrade our habits, and optimize our lives — just like updating a system?

Here's how:

- **Memory** improves when we organize information like a well-structured hard drive.
- **Focus** sharpens when we eliminate distractions — just like closing unnecessary apps.
- **Habits** become automatic when we train our brains to run them in the background, like software.

- **Health** thrives when we track and refine our inputs — food, sleep, and movement — like a system upgrade.

Instead of taking control, we often allow external influences — social media, advertising, and peer pressure — to dictate our thoughts, emotions, and behaviors. We react instead of programming ourselves.

When you become the programmer of your own mind, everything changes.

- You make deliberate choices instead of reacting on impulse.
- Your actions align with long-term success rather than short-term gratification.
- You move through life with clarity, precision, and control.

The world won't slow down, but you can decide how you process it. That's exactly what this book will teach you.

There are people—monks, yogis, spiritual masters—who can meditate to such an extent that their bodies enter altered states. Some appear to defy gravity. Others can slow their heart rate, resist extreme cold, or enter deep states of awareness where pain and fear no longer exist. These aren't myths. They've been documented by scientists, but what if these abilities are just the surface of what's possible? Ancient stories speak of miracles—parting the sea, walking on water, turning water into wine. Most people view these as religious symbols or metaphors. But there's another way to look at it. What if the human brain, when completely aligned with the body and spirit, is capable of interacting with the physical world in ways we don't yet understand?

We already know the placebo effect is real. We know that belief can affect biology. We know that our thoughts change our chemistry. So the question is: if the mind can influence the body, can it also influence the world around us?

Maybe parting the sea wasn't about magic it was about complete focus, clarity, and presence. Maybe turning water into wine wasn't about illusion—it was about pure intention and belief at a level we can't yet replicate.

The brain is more than a tool for solving problems or storing memories. It might be a transmitter, a receiver, and a creative force. Most people use it for routine survival. A few train it like a muscle, push it to the edge, and discover what it can really do.

These ancient stories could be early records of what happens when a person is fully aligned—physically, mentally, and spiritually. Not supernatural. Just natural at a level we haven't reached yet.

You don't need to walk on water, but you do need to stop walking through life full of doubt. Because doubt is the only thing that blocks power.

This isn't about rigid rules. **It's about a framework—one that adapts to you, wherever you are in life.**

Whether you're a student, a parent, an entrepreneur, or someone simply looking for balance, this system will work for you.

Each chapter will break down **key principles** and show you exactly **how to apply them.**

Here's what we'll cover:

- **Mindset & Mental Clarity** – Programming your subconscious for success.
- **Health & Fitness** – Optimizing your body with simple, effective habits.
- **Relationships & Family** – Building deep, meaningful connections.

- **Productivity & Learning** – Operating at peak efficiency every day.
- **Wealth & Financial Freedom** – Mastering money and escaping consumerism.

This isn't another self-help book filled with vague advice.

It's a **manual for life**—designed to cut through the noise and give you a **real, practical system**, because you don't need more motivation.

You need a system that works, and that's exactly what this book is about.

Training Your Brain: From Conscious to Subconscious

At the risk of sounding atheist to some, religious to others, or perhaps even a little unconventional, I'm still going to go down this discussion—because it's worth considering.

You know how ancient wisdom was often passed on through allegories, designed to preserve deeper messages across generations? What if the story of Adam and Eve isn't just a literal event, but an allegory meant to explain something far more profound?

What if the forbidden fruit was not just an act of disobedience, but a representation of a pivotal shift in human evolution—perhaps a genetic change, a biological or neurological trigger that separated the cognitive brain from the subconscious mind, replacing instinct and blind trust in the process with self-awareness and doubt?

Most religions emphasize trust in God, belief in a higher force, the idea that God is everywhere. But what if this is another way of describing something that science is just beginning to understand—that our subconscious minds are interconnected in an invisible, energetic web? That trusting "God" simply means trusting the process of life itself, allowing this unseen intelligence to guide us?

I'm not here to prove or disprove the existence of God. That debate has raged on for centuries. But I do acknowledge that something larger than the individual human exists. Maybe it's the vast intelligence of the universe, the subconscious collective, or an unseen field that connects us all.

Faith, in any form, is a way to surrender to the process—whether through prayer, meditation, or spiritual belief in something greater than ourselves.

Whatever it is, the key is learning how to work with it.

Every religion, in one way or another, incorporates a form of prayer or meditation. Some kneel, some repeat sacred words, others engage in rhythmic chants, and some use movement or symbolic rituals. While these practices vary in form, their purpose is strikingly similar across cultures and belief systems: **to quiet the internal dialogue and embed desires, hopes, and intentions into the subconscious mind.**

At its core, prayer is **not just about speaking to a deity—it's about reprogramming the mind.** The words, movements, and rituals help cut through the noise of daily thoughts, **entraining the subconscious mind to focus on certain desires, emotions, and goals.** Whether someone views this as spiritual or psychological, the effect is real.

Charles Aznavour's story is a perfect example of the subconscious mind's power in shaping reality. Lacking the conventional looks and voice of a singer, he faced countless rejections, yet he held onto his unwavering conviction. After years of struggle, nearly bankrupt and on the verge of giving up, he took the stage one last time and sang **Je m'voyais déjà**, a song about an artist dreaming of success, but in that moment, something extraordinary happened—he lost himself in his subconscious vision, fully immersing in the dream he had carried for so long. He sang not with doubt or hesitation, but with the energy of someone who already was the artist he envisioned. His mind, body, and emotions aligned completely with his belief. The audience, initially skeptical, felt the raw authenticity of his performance, and that single moment became the turning point of his career. This is the power of the subconscious—when the mind fully commits to a vision with absolute certainty, reality follows. Aznavour, once dismissed as an outsider, transformed into one of the greatest singers of his time, proving that when you embody your dream completely, the world eventually sees what you've always known deep inside.

The goal of this book is to train your brain to seamlessly shift thoughts, ideas, and desires from the conscious mind to the subconscious—just as a computer or search engine processes queries in the background while you continue working. But beyond that, my attempt is to bridge the gap between ancient wisdom and modern life. For centuries, knowledge has been passed down through generations—through rituals, proverbs, and traditions designed to shape the mind, body, and spirit. These timeless principles, though often overlooked in today's fast-paced world, hold the key to living with clarity, balance, and purpose. By understanding and integrating both the wisdom of the past and the efficiency of modern systems, we can create a life that is not just productive, but truly fulfilling.

Think about how a GPS navigator works. You input a destination, and it calculates the best route. Once you start driving, it quietly monitors your progress, recalibrating in real time—suggesting shortcuts, avoiding roadblocks, and adapting to traffic conditions. You don't manually reassess your route every second; the system does it for you.

Your brain is capable of the same efficiency. When you consciously decide on a goal—whether it's improving your health, mastering a skill, or building financial stability—you need to program it into your subconscious. The active mind should focus on the present moment: working, studying, exercising, living. Meanwhile, in the background, your subconscious gathers data, makes connections, and presents you with insights and solutions when the time is right.

Too many people overburden their conscious mind, trying to hold onto every detail, every task, every outcome. This leads to overwhelm, anxiety, and inaction. Instead, the key is to delegate. Let your subconscious mind take over the processing while you focus on executing what's in front of you.

The Lord's Prayer holds a timeless message that goes far beyond religion—it offers a mindset for life. It invites you to give thanks for what you already have, to focus only on "our daily bread"—the essentials of today—and to trust that everything else will unfold as it should. In essence, it's a call to be grateful, to stay present, and to release the need for control. When you focus on the task at hand and let go of future anxieties, you allow your subconscious to do what it does best: process, align, and guide you forward. True peace comes not from planning every outcome, but from trusting that you're already on the right path.

Here's how it works:

- Set a clear goal or intention. Write it down, visualize it, and then let it go.
- Shift your focus to immediate actions—reading, working, exercising, learning.

Trust that your subconscious will organize the information and present the best path forward.

By doing this, you are essentially hacking your own operating system. You're allowing your mind to work in the background, filtering unnecessary noise while keeping your deeper ambitions alive and active. Just like a search engine, it will deliver the best results—if you give it the right input and let it run without interference.

Master this, and you'll never again feel stuck or overwhelmed. Instead, your mind will become a tool of precision—navigating life's complexities with ease, clarity, and purpose.

Sometimes, the inability to program your brain to follow through on a plan isn't just about discipline—it's because, you're stuck worrying about something. That worry acts as mental resistance, making it impossible to push forward until it's addressed. Just like a computer running a complex Excel formula, if your system starts lagging or freezing, you can't simply switch to another task and expect everything to run smoothly. You either need to let the process finish or force a shutdown.

But here's the catch—forcing a shutdown might not fully solve the issue. When you restart, the same problem could persist, requiring a deeper fix before everything runs efficiently again.

The same applies to the brain. Shutting down—meaning attempting to push a problem away—won't work, because your mind will keep running in circles, trying to process what was left unresolved. Here's how to do it effectively...If something is weighing on you, approach it like a trial—gather all the evidence, present your strongest defence, and accept the verdict with peace. Do everything within your power to resolve the situation in your mind, be brutally honest with yourself in the process, and once you've given it your best effort, let it go. Holding onto worry beyond that point serves no purpose; it only drains your energy and keeps you in a loop of hesitation. True progress happens when your mind is clear, free from unresolved concerns that quietly sabotage your focus. Face what's bothering you, handle it with intention, and once you've done all you can, shift your attention forward—because only then can you fully commit to the path ahead.

Your brain is like an advanced operating system—it runs background processes you don't see. The key is learning how to program it deliberately instead of letting outdated scripts run your life

- Your **subconscious** is the **processor**, working constantly in the background.
- Your **conscious mind** is the **screen**, displaying whatever is currently running.

Everything you think, say, and believe **programs your subconscious**, shaping your behavior and the outcomes in your life.
This isn't magic—it's simply how the mind operates.

For example:

Instead of forcing yourself into a state of **artificial motivation** or drowning in **decision fatigue**, sometimes the best approach is to **step back** and allow your subconscious to process information in the background.
Instead of resisting a task with thoughts like:
- Ugh, I don't want to work out
- I really don't feel like going to the grocery store.

Shift the narrative to something **neutral or curious**:
- Should I wear the sweat pants, or shorts would be more comfortable
- Maybe I'll grab some walnuts; they'd be great for my diet.

This **small mental shift removes resistance** and turns tasks from **obligations into** choices.

The goal isn't to fake excitement—it's to **reduce the time of processing.**

Breaking the Cycle: Reprogramming Addiction and Habits

Smoking is a perfect example. Most people try to quit smoking the wrong way. They tell themselves, "After **this pack, I'm done,"** but in reality, they're focused on finishing the pack. Meanwhile, their body—already dependent on nicotine—keeps demanding more, and the cycle continues.

The same applies to **food.** If you constantly think, **"I should eat healthy,"** your mind stays fixated on food. You eat something unhealthy, feel guilty, then compensate by eating something nutritious—only to repeat the cycle. This back-and-forth creates a mental loop that leads to frustration rather than progress.

So, how do you change the process? By keeping your mind engaged and focusing on fulfilling, purposeful activities. Don't expect overnight success—just as your bad habits developed gradually, good ones will take time to build as well.

The key isn't just to stop a habit—it's to replace it. Your brain craves stimulation, so give it something equally engaging, something that excites you as much as the habit you're trying to quit. Whether it's smoking, junk food, or any other self-destructive cycle, you need to redirect that energy toward something productive.

Obsession isn't the enemy—misplaced obsession is. The trick is to rewire your mind to crave progress instead of stagnation. When your focus shifts to something that genuinely fulfills you, the old habit starts to lose its grip. Over time, without force or struggle, you'll find yourself naturally outgrowing what no longer serves you.

How to Accelerate This Process

Reprogram your brain intentionally.

- Instead of blaming yourself for smoking, accept that you are actively reprogramming a habit.
- Spend a few minutes daily reflecting on why life is better without cigarettes.
- Visualize the benefits—saving money, fresher breath, glowing skin, more stamina.
- Focus on becoming a non-smoker rather than forcing yourself to quit.

This process applies to everything in life—whether it's breaking bad habits, building success, or strengthening relationships. Once you learn how to consciously program your brain, you take control over your actions and outcomes.

A Simple Trick: Reprogramming Through Passwords

One of the easiest ways to reshape your subconscious is through **passwords as affirmations.**

Think about it—every day, you type in passwords for your phone, email, work accounts. Why not turn this into a tool for self-improvement?

Try this:

Instead of random words, create a **password that reinforces your goal.** Use a phrase like "IAmHealthy2022!" or "Icandoit$$$"—but spell it in another language or add unique symbols to keep it secure. Every time you type it, your brain processes that message, reinforcing the belief. Over time, this repetition subtly **reprograms your subconscious.**

This method works for any habit whether it's quitting smoking, improving self-discipline, or shifting your mindset toward success. The more you **see, say, and engage with a thought,** the more it becomes embedded in your identity.

When I was in my 30s and newly settled in a new country, my English was basic at best. Navigating life in a different culture was already a challenge, but I was determined to progress in my career. To do that, I needed to pass several professional exams — exams that would have been complicated even for native English speakers. For me, whose fourth language was English, they felt almost impossible. I remember enrolling in one particular course and receiving the textbook. As I flipped through the pages, it felt like I was reading gibberish. The words blurred together, and frustration quickly set in. Every chapter seemed like an insurmountable wall, but there was one small thing that kept me going. My password to access these courses was simple yet powerful: **ICANDOIT**. Every time I typed it, I wasn't just logging in — I was programming my brain to believe in my abilities. Each keystroke became a quiet declaration of confidence, a reminder that I was capable, resilient, and determined to succeed.

Slowly but surely, I pushed through the confusion. I studied, I stumbled, and I kept typing that password. ICANDOIT. And, I did!

Manifestation vs. Programming

You've probably heard the term *manifesting* — it's all over social media.

Every few years, it becomes trendy again, and suddenly, platforms are flooded with people teaching you how to "manifest your dream life." I've read plenty of books on it myself, and most of them offer the same generic advice:

Steps to Manifest:

• Find the right time.
• Do some breathing exercises.
• Calm and quiet your mind.

Sounds complicated, doesn't it?

Here's the truth — it's not really about manifesting. It's about **programming.**

All those steps assume you have endless time and energy to devote to rituals, but most people don't. Life is busy and sitting down to "align your vibrations" often feels unrealistic. The good news? You don't need elaborate ceremonies to create the life you want.

What you do need is:

• A clear, persistent vision of your goals.

- The discipline to keep that vision in your subconscious mind for ongoing processing.

It's not about wishing for something and waiting for the universe to deliver. It's a physical, intentional effort — a continuous act of programming your brain. That's how real change happens.

A Classic Example: Gone with the Wind

In *Gone with the Wind by Margaret Mitchell*, Scarlett O'Hara's famous line:
"I can't think about that right now. If I do, I'll go crazy. I'll think about that tomorrow."
captures a **powerful instinctive response** to overwhelming emotions.
Rather than allowing herself to be paralyzed by anxiety, Scarlett:
Postpones emotional processing.
Pushes the burden from her conscious mind to her subconscious.
This isn't avoidance—it's a form of resilience.
She understands that **dwelling on a problem won't solve it immediately**, so she places it in the background, trusting that **when the time is right, she'll know exactly how to handle it.**
One of the most well-known instances of this is **near the end of the book** when she refuses to accept the reality of **Rhett Butler leaving her.**
Instead of spiraling into emotional despair, she defers her pain and tells herself she'll come up with a plan later.

It's a pattern seen all too often—and it raises a deeper question: *why do some people succeed while others struggle*? The answer lies in conditioning. Some people change, while others remain stuck, because many let external influences dictate their internal programming. They adopt limiting beliefs, follow societal expectations, and live with self-doubt, never realising they have the power to rewrite their own code. You've probably heard the phrase "ignorance is bliss," and in some cases, there's truth to it. Highly educated people often have ten answers to the same question, analyzing every possibility, weighing every outcome—sometimes to the point of paralysis. Meanwhile, those with less knowledge may only have one answer, giving them fewer variables to consider and making decision-making much simpler. So here's the thing—either you've reached a level of gaining full control over your subconscious mind, or you're blissfully unaware, convinced you have all the answers without realizing how much you don't know.

Success isn't about intelligence, luck, or background—it's about having a clear vision and refusing to let distractions pull you off course.

This is the foundation of everything I'll teach you in this book.

- How to program your brain to think in ways that lead to success.
- How to break bad habits and form good ones without struggle.
- How to eliminate mental clutter and focus on what truly matters.

Life isn't complicated—we just make it that way, but once you learn to simplify your thoughts, you can simplify your actions, and when you simplify your actions, success becomes inevitable.

Simply put, here's what we're aiming to achieve—and this isn't just a metaphor. This is how your mind should be programmed. You are the screenwriter, the director, the actor, and the producer of your own life. Every scene, every decision, every turning point is yours to shape. Wealth, status, or circumstance aren't prerequisites for a fulfilling existence—your mindset is. By the time we reach adulthood, we've seen enough films to understand that life isn't a predictable, straight-line story. It's filled with highs and lows, love and heartbreak, breakthroughs and breakdowns. So instead of resisting the chaos, embrace it. Right now, you might feel like you're living in *The Pursuit of Happiness*—and that's okay. But here's the shift: don't just relate to the story. Rewrite it. Imagine a new ending in your mind every night before you fall asleep. Replay it again and again, editing the scenes, adjusting the tone, strengthening the outcome. The more you visualise it, the more your subconscious aligns with that reality. You're not just playing a role—you're directing every scene. And whatever genre life throws at you next—romance, adventure, redemption— remember, you are both the storyteller and the main character. So write something worth watching.

Lifelong Project

You are not a moment, not a phase,
Not a list of habits set ablaze.
You are a work in progress, a moving tide,
A story unfolding, not set aside.
Don't wait for storms to shift your way,
For loss or love to spark the day.
Why wait for triggers, for time to demand,
When growth is already in your hand?
Evolve with purpose, steady, strong,
Change doesn't come from waiting long.

Improve, refine, let each day show,

That joy is found in how you grow.

Anna Izmirlian

Step 1: Balance Your Body Before Programming Your Mind

Health & Personal Responsibility

Everything you're about to read comes from years of trial and error—my own body, my own mind, and my own relentless curiosity. I've spent countless hours digging through books, experimenting with routines, and pushing myself through both good and bad decisions. I'm not a doctor. I'm not here to diagnose or prescribe. I'm simply sharing what actually worked for me—what made me feel stronger, clearer, more alive.

If you're dealing with health issues or have unique needs, talk to someone you trust in the medical world. Use your judgment. This isn't about replacing professional care—it's about realizing how much power you already have. More than you think. Possibly more than anyone ever told you. Because once you start taking ownership of your well-being, things begin to shift. Slowly at first, then all at once.

While doctors and medical professionals provide essential expertise, your daily choices—what you eat, how you move, how you manage stress—shape your health in powerful ways. Taking ownership of your body and lifestyle is not about replacing professional guidance but about realizing the impact of your own decisions.

Before we get started, let's get one thing clear: **you are a complex machine—a system of chemicals, minerals, and electrical signals running through your body.** Your brain is not separate from your body. It is an organ, just like your heart or liver, and it functions based on the **fuel** and **conditions** you provide. If your physical body isn't functioning well, your brain isn't operating at full capacity. And if your brain isn't operating at full capacity, you **won't** be able to program it properly.

I say this with full awareness that some people face illnesses or conditions that cannot be changed. This book is not about unrealistic perfection. It's about **understanding your personal capacity and building on it.** Whatever your situation—whether you are perfectly healthy, struggling with an imbalance, or dealing with a condition beyond your control—the goal is the same: **optimize yourself to the best of your ability.**

Start With Blood Work—Your Personal System Scan

Before we talk about habits, discipline, success, or mental strength, the first thing you need to do is **get a full blood workup.**

This means testing for:

- **Vitamin & Mineral Levels** – Deficiencies in iron, magnesium, B12, or vitamin D can affect your mood, energy, and ability to focus.
- **Hormone Levels** – Your body's balance of testosterone, estrogen, cortisol, and thyroid hormones has a **massive impact** on your emotions, motivation, and decision-making.

- **Blood Sugar & Insulin Levels** – Unstable blood sugar leads to energy crashes, poor concentration, and increased stress.
- **Inflammation Markers** – Chronic inflammation is linked to fatigue, brain fog, and mental health struggles.

Even if you look healthy and feel fine on the surface, if you struggle with self-control, anxiety, anger, or bad habits, it could be **a chemical imbalance, not a willpower problem.**

For example:

You're in great shape but have **a bad habit of biting your nails or picking at your skin**—this could be linked to **mineral deficiencies or anxiety triggered by imbalances in your nervous system.**
You get **easily frustrated, short-tempered, or emotionally drained**—this could be **hormonal or a sign of nutrient depletion.**
These things are **not just personality traits**—they are **symptoms.** And like any system, before you fix the software (your thoughts and habits), you need to **check the hardware (your body).**

Now, let's make one thing clear: this book is written so that anyone—at any life stage, in any financial situation—can apply these ideas.

- **Get your blood work done.** In many countries, basic tests are covered by healthcare systems or can be done affordably through clinics.
- **Identify imbalances.** If you can afford it, see a **naturopath or homeopath** to get a deeper understanding of your body's balance.

- **If that's not an option, focus on diet.** The easiest way to start balancing your body is through **proper nutrition.**

Think about it: if we are **machines made of chemicals and minerals**, then what we **fuel** ourselves with directly affects our function.

At the most basic level, you need to:

- Eat all major food groups—protein, fats, carbohydrates, vitamins, and minerals.
- Reduce ultra-processed foods—your body cannot function optimally on artificial fuel.
- Stay hydrated—dehydration leads to brain fog, mood swings, and fatigue.

The goal isn't to follow a strict diet. The goal is balance.

Long before modern science uncovered the importance of gut health, religious and philosophical traditions emphasized dietary principles that align with what we now understand about digestion. These ancient teachings may not have explicitly mentioned gut microbiota, but they advocated for moderation, fasting, natural foods, and mindful consumption—all essential for a healthy digestive system.

The **Bible** outlines dietary laws in Leviticus and Deuteronomy to help ancient communities avoid harmful bacteria, while Proverbs and Corinthians promote mindful eating. **Ayurveda**, rooted in Hinduism, introduces the concept of Agni (digestive fire), recommending fasting and a Sattvic diet filled with gut-friendly foods. **Buddhist texts** reinforce mindful eating and fasting, emphasizing simplicity and awareness for better health.

In **Islam**, the Quran encourages consuming only Tayyib (pure) foods, practicing moderation, and engaging in fasting—practices now linked to improved gut microbiome diversity. **Jewish traditions**, including Kosher laws and Talmudic teachings, regulate food purity and stress intentional eating. **Taoist philosophy**, as described in The Yellow Emperor's Classic of Medicine, connects digestion to overall energy balance.

These ancient traditions reflect an intuitive understanding of health—guiding people toward digestion-friendly habits long before modern research confirmed their benefits.

Research suggests that infants and young children naturally regulate their hunger and satiety signals. However, exposure to highly processed foods early in life can disrupt these instincts, leading to cravings and unhealthy eating habits. Over time, their ability to self-regulate diminishes, leading to poor eating habits, nutritional imbalances, and long-term health issues.

Rather than trusting their instincts, we override them for convenience. The result? A generation struggling with energy, focus, and well-being—not because their bodies failed them, but because we disrupted the very mechanisms designed to keep them in balance.

In my experience, that reset can happen at any age. I struggled with digestive issues for a while, until I realised that healing wasn't always about doing more—it was about giving my body the space to do what it was designed to do. Sometimes, the most powerful medicine is rest. Fasting, when done periodically, became a gentle way for me to step back and let my body recover and rebalance itself naturally.

Much of this wisdom, I owe to my grandmother—my best friend, my rock. From a young age, she introduced me to the beauty of simple, nourishing food. While other kids reached for chocolate and ice cream, I looked forward to her homemade Swiss chard soup. That early exposure to natural, wholesome meals didn't just shape my palate—it shaped my body's chemistry in ways I'll always be grateful for.

She didn't just teach me how to eat well; she passed down nature's medicine. Sea buckthorn, raw honey, chamomile—remedies used for centuries before they became wellness trends. There was a time when people relied on nature to heal, nourish, and thrive, but somewhere along the way, capitalism erased this wisdom from our lives, replacing it with quick fixes, processed foods, and chemical-laden solutions. The truth is, the more we reconnect with natural ways of living, the better we feel— physically, mentally, and emotionally. My grandmother understood this long before it was trendy. And for that, I am forever grateful.

While modern medicine has made incredible advancements in treating diseases, many of us have lost touch with basic health principles—nutrition, movement, sleep, and stress management. Preventative care should be a foundation, not an afterthought.

The Power of Sleep: Why You Should Never Sacrifice It

For most of my life, I maintained a stable weight and good health. Then life changed. My sleep dropped from a consistent eight hours a night to unpredictable, broken rest.

The results were immediate:

- My **health declined**.
- I became **less patient** and more irritable.
- I gained **weight**.

Sleep isn't just rest—it's your body's built-in reset mechanism. During deep sleep, your brain flushes out metabolic waste, acting as a self-cleaning system. Without proper sleep:

- Mental clarity declines.
- Emotional regulation becomes harder.
- Your body retains unnecessary waste, leading to weight gain and sluggishness.

There's a reason people say 'sleep on it.' With around 90% of our brain's activity happening on a subconscious level, sleep provides the perfect opportunity for your mind to process, reset, and often arrive at solutions you couldn't see the night before."

How to Optimize Your Sleep:

- **Avoid Coffee & Alcohol Before Bed** Caffeine and alcohol dehydrate the brain and disrupt deep sleep. Your body needs water for detoxification, just like the Earth relies on water for renewal.
- **Respect Your Body's Detox Cycle** Sleep is like internal photosynthesis—a chemical process crucial for restoration. Poor sleep disrupts this, leading to brain fog, sluggishness, and hormonal imbalances.
- **Hydrate First Thing in the Morning** Sleep is a period of overnight dehydration. Replenish with water and a pinch of natural salt to restore electrolytes.
- **Use Natural Supplements if Necessary** Magnesium, melatonin, or herbal teas can support deep sleep.
- **Create a bedtime routine** that signals your brain to wind down.

Depression in layman's terms

While focusing on our physical well-being is important, we often overlook our mindset. For a long time, I experienced what I can only describe as a form of depression. I was never formally diagnosed, but if I had sought professional help, I'm fairly certain that label would have applied. Looking back, I see that those feelings were often triggered by circumstances that left me feeling stuck, unfulfilled, or disconnected.

Mental health is complex, and professionals undoubtedly have a deeper understanding of depression than I do. But from my personal experience, I've noticed it can stem from several sources:

- **Chemical Imbalances:** Biological factors that may require medical support.
- **Unfulfillment:** Reflecting on past choices with disappointment.
- **Grief and Loss:** The overwhelming sadness that follows the death of a loved one.

Much of the inadequacy we feel stems from competition. And today, that competition is no longer just with our neighbours—it's with thousands of strangers on social media. We're constantly racing against people, against time, measuring our worth by asking, *"What have I achieved so far?"*

We're born into a world that hands us a script:
Go to school. Get a job. Get married. Have children. Retire.
Deviate from that path, and suddenly life feels harder.
Not because you've done anything wrong—but because you've been programmed to believe that you have.

But what if your purpose was never meant to follow that script?

What if you were here to create, to awaken others, to heal pain no one else could see, or to quietly shift the course of a generation?

And just because you haven't achieved certain milestones by their timeline doesn't mean you haven't accomplished something extraordinary.

We compare ourselves as if we're all climbing the same staircase—

But some people begin on step 78.

Others, like you, may have started at step negative 50, buried beneath inherited trauma, generational cycles, or simply the weight of being different.

So if that person now stands at step 150, and you're at 145—

don't forget that you've climbed nearly 200 steps to get there.

That's not just success—that's transcendence.

Struggle isn't always failure.

Sometimes, it's resistance showing up when you begin walking away from programming and towards your true path—the one no one told you existed, because it was meant to be forged by you.

And here's something else we forget: life doesn't end at 20, 30, or 40.

Yes, it *can*—but we don't know that.

The only certainty we have is the present moment.

So why not pour your energy into doing your best *now*, instead of worrying about what you may or may not have a year from today?

Here's a simple truth: happiness isn't found in some grand destination. It's tucked quietly into the present—the moments we overlook while chasing something bigger.

Try this: for one week, live entirely in the now.

Measure your life not by achievements, but by experiences.

A warm, flavourful meal at your favourite restaurant.

The laughter of good company.

A long, hot shower with perfect water pressure.

The scent of fresh air, the taste of morning coffee, the quiet satisfaction of a task well done.

Focus fully on each act—not tomorrow, not yesterday—just this one thing, done with intention, done with joy.

Make it your practice: to be fully present, fully alive. One moment at a time.

Do this, and you'll realise... happiness isn't hiding. It's right here, waiting for you to notice.

Not every chapter of your life will be filled with passion and purpose. Sometimes, you're simply doing what you must—getting by while waiting for something more meaningful to take shape.

But even in those moments, happiness isn't out of reach.

If you're working a job that doesn't fulfil you, one that feels far from your calling, you can still choose to live moment to moment.

Notice the small wins—a kind interaction, your favourite playlist in the background, the way sunlight filters through a window.

The rhythm of the work.

A good coffee on your break.

A deep breath between tasks.

You're still here. You're still moving forward.

This chapter won't last forever. But how you show up for it will shape what comes next.

Practice presence.

Pour love into the now, even if it's not where you want to stay.

The door to the next stage often opens when you've mastered gratitude in the one you're in.

One of the biggest reasons we feel inadequate is because we're not only competing with others—we're competing with time itself.

In the past, people may not have labelled depression the way we do today, but they often had a stronger sense of purpose and community.

Those human connections gave them resilience during difficult times.

While it's essential to acknowledge and address depression, it's just as important to understand where it stems from.

The more we reinforce the belief that we're "depressed," the harder it becomes to break free from that identity.

But real healing often begins with small, deliberate actions: movement, connection, purpose, and structure.

These simple steps can reset the mind and help us reclaim a sense of control.

No matter where you're starting from, there is an ideal version of you—and your role is to move as close to that version as possible.

This isn't about chasing perfection or meeting unrealistic standards.

It's about defining what *your* best looks like:

- If you struggle with low energy, the ideal version of you has steady, sustainable energy.
- If you experience mood swings, the ideal version of you feels emotionally balanced.
- If you feel stuck, the ideal version of you is engaged, curious, and fulfilled.

What Comes Next? Balancing the Mind

At this point, you've done the most critical step: you've balanced your body.

- Your **vitamins and minerals** are at optimal levels.
- Your **hormones** are stable.
- You're **eating real food** and **drinking enough water**.

Now, we can move to the real work: **programming your mind**.

Because here's the truth:

Even with a perfectly healthy body, you can still be mentally stuck.

The next step is learning how to take control of your brain:

- **How to stop overthinking**
- **How to break bad habits**
- **How to rewire your subconscious for success**

Most people fail at self-improvement because they try to fix their mind while ignoring their body. But now, you know the truth:

Everything starts with balance.

Step 2: Understanding Your Mind Before Programming It

Now that your body is balanced and functioning at its best, it's time for the next critical step: **clearing out the noise and understanding what you truly want.**

This is where most people get stuck. They think they know what they want, but in reality, their desires are a mix of social expectations, external pressures, and habits they've picked up along the way. That's why, despite reaching career goals, making money, and ticking off life's milestones, **so few people are genuinely happy.** They followed a script that wasn't theirs. Before you can start living a **structured, intentional life**, you need to know **what you actually want.** Not what your parents wanted for you. Not what your friends expect. Not what society considers "successful."

You need **your own voice** to be the loudest one in your head.

In my late 40s, as I reflected on my life, I realised two things: everything I had ever wanted—everything I had once programmed my mind with—had quietly become my reality. Anyone who knows me would say I have an excellent memory. I can recall the exact moments when those thoughts, those desires, were first planted. But here's what I didn't see at the time: I hadn't wanted the *right* things. I had programmed myself with limitations inherited from my upbringing. Deep down, I didn't believe I deserved more.

And that's where everything began to shift.

For a moment, close your eyes.

Forget your looks.

Forget your gender, your skin colour, your past.

Let go of the stories you've been told—stories of hardship, of belonging or rejection, of rights given or denied.

Imagine yourself as something simpler.

An organism.

A being that has never been programmed by the world's expectations.

A blank slate.

Picture a brand-new computer, its screen glowing for the first time, ready to be installed with fresh software.

No preloaded stories. No corrupted files.

Just infinite possibilities.

Now ask yourself—what kind of life would you choose to build?

What values would you install?

What apps would you run?

As you define that vision, let everything that doesn't belong simply fade away.

The voices that told you you're not enough.

The hands that withheld opportunity.

The weight of other people's fears and judgments.

Forget it.

And now—imagine walking through the world without any labels at all.

Pretend, just for a moment, that when people look at you, they don't see where you came from.

They don't see your background, your name, your face.

They see a presence. A force. A creature of potential.

Something extraordinary, evolving in real time.

Not someone boxed in by roles or appearance—but someone breaking patterns.

Someone who isn't here to impress, but to impact.

They don't see restrictions.

They see possibilities.

They don't seek to criticize you.

They're drawn to your courage, your light.

They want to support you, love you, uplift you.

Let that be the energy you walk with.

It's hard, I know.

But as Buddha said, "With our thoughts, we build the world around us."

And that world—*your* world—is yours to shape.

Start acting like someone who's been given a second chance at life.

A person who no longer identifies by the labels given at birth,

but by the limitless potential of their existence.

Live as an organism that wants to create, to build, to love, to flourish.

Let *that* be your identity—not one assigned by others,

but one designed by you.

Take Time Alone in Nature: Reconnect With Yourself: A Day in Solitude

Set aside half a day—or even better, a full day   to be alone in nature.

- No phone.
- No social media.
- No conversations.
- Just you and your thoughts.

If possible, walk barefoot. Feel the earth beneath you. Let the silence take over. Let your thoughts settle.

This isn't about pushing your body or forcing yourself into meditation. It's about stepping away from the noise of everyday life so you can finally hear yourself think. If you can afford it, consider spending a week at a secluded mountain resort— somewhere with fresh air, breathtaking views, and complete quiet—to fully disconnect, reset your mind, and gain deeper clarity.

For centuries, monks and spiritual seekers have retreated to the mountains to seek clarity, wisdom, and inner peace. High-altitude monasteries like Montserrat in Spain or Meteora in Greece weren't built on mountain peaks by accident—they were intentionally placed where the distractions of the world couldn't reach. Away from the chaos, in a space where the air is crisp and the silence is uninterrupted, the mind has room to expand.

While there, ask yourself:

- What do I actually love?

- What makes me feel alive?

- What do I value most in life?

- Who do I love?

- How do I feel about my relationships?

- Which of my dreams are truly mine, and which were given to me by society?

The Subconscious Desire Test

Sometimes, the clearest path to understanding what we truly want isn't found through logic—it's found in instinct. This reflective exercise is inspired by symbolic association work found in Jungian psychology and adapted from various subconscious awareness practices.

Don't overthink. Let your answers flow naturally. There are no wrong responses— only insight.

1. What is your favourite animal?
Describe it in three to five words. Think about how it makes you feel, how it moves, the energy it gives off.
This symbolizes the qualities you subconsciously seek in a romantic partner. It reflects the energy you're drawn to—the traits you crave in someone you could build a life with.

2. What is your second favourite animal?
Describe it in three to five words.
This represents how you see yourself—your core personality, your identity, how you move through the world when you're most aligned.

3. What is your favourite body of water?

Ocean, river, lake, stream, waterfall—choose one, and describe it in three to five words.

This reflects your subconscious attitude toward sex and sensuality. The depth, movement, energy, or stillness of the water mirrors your intimate desires and emotional flow.

4. What is your favourite colour?

Describe it in three to five words.

This reveals how you see your overall personality—your emotional tone, your vibe, the kind of presence you carry without even trying.

5. What is your favourite type of weather?

Sunny, stormy, crisp autumn air, quiet snowfall… describe it in three to five words.

This represents your deeper attitude toward life itself—how you move through the world, what you value, and how you experience the rhythm of your days.

When you're done, look back.

Does it align with the life you're living now—or the one you're still craving?

What you see here might surprise you.

Or… it might just confirm what you already knew deep down.

Let's put this into perspective.

Do you truly want a five-bedroom house with a big backyard?

Or do you want it because society equates it with success?

Maybe, in reality, you'd be happier in a sleek penthouse with a breathtaking view and no maintenance. Maybe you'd rather spend your time traveling than taking care of a large home.

This is why so many people chase things that never truly satisfy them. They think they want something—only to get it and feel empty.

And then what happens?

- They reach a certain level in their career but still feel unfulfilled.
- They settle down with someone they don't love because "it made sense."
- They accumulate everything they thought they wanted—yet they're miserable.

People struggle with happiness not because they're incapable of finding it, but because they never stop to ask themselves what would actually fulfill them.

The good news? You don't have to make that mistake. You can start uncovering what you truly want—right now.

If one day alone isn't enough to gain clarity, take more time.

Most people never spend real time alone with their thoughts. They drown themselves in distractions—TV shows, Social Media, background noise—because they're afraid of hearing their own voice, but that little voice? It's there.

One of my favourite moments in The Road to El Dorado is when Tulio turns to Miguel and says:

"Let's pretend for a second you have that little voice. What does it tell you?"

Even though this doesn't directly apply to what I'm saying, I find it funny—and oddly relevant.

You do have that little voice.

The problem is, it's been buried under too much information, too much technology, and too many outside opinions.

That's why this step is essential. You need solitude—real, uninterrupted solitude—to filter out the noise and uncover what actually matters to you.

Revisiting the First Two Steps Before Moving Forward

Let's go back, because these first two steps are everything.

- **Get your blood work done.** Don't just depend on **friends' advice, social media trends, or the latest health craze** telling you which supplements are "life-changing." Just because something worked for someone else doesn't mean it's what **your body** needs. Before you start adding vitamins or making drastic health changes, **get tested** for deficiencies and hormonal imbalances.
- **Fix deficiencies & seek expert guidance.** If you need a **doctor, naturopath, or homeopath—go.** Your health is not a guessing game. Social media might tell you that a particular vitamin is "essential," but the truth is, taking unnecessary supplements can do more harm than good. Get professional advice based on **your** body's specific needs, not just what's trending.
- **Understand your mind.** Take time in solitude to disconnect from external expectations and uncover your true desires.

Once you have these two pieces in place, we can begin the real work.

Programming Begins Now

Most people are so caught up in outside demands, fleeting thoughts, and endless distractions that they can't even hear their own voice. The are reacting to life instead of creating it.

But now? You have a balanced body. You have a clear understanding of what you actually want.

This is where things shift.

It's time to reprogram your mind—step by step.

And trust me, once you start doing this, your entire life will transform.

Step 3—How to Program Your Brain for Success

We're about to take everything we've done so far and use it to **build the life you actually want**—not the one society tells you to live.

This is where we **delete old programs** and install **new, more powerful ones**.

Get ready.

Your environment is an extension of your mind. If your space is cluttered, your **thoughts will be cluttered**. If your wardrobe is chaotic, your **daily routine will be chaotic**. Programming your brain is **only as good as the commands you give it**, and if your subconscious is constantly distracted by unnecessary stimuli, you are wasting energy without even realizing it.

This step is about **eliminating distractions**, both physically and mentally, to create an environment that supports focus, clarity, and success.

Step 3A: The Power of a Clear Space and a Clear Mind

I've moved nine or ten times, and each time, I was confronted with a harsh truth — I had far too much stuff. Every box I packed was a reminder of unnecessary accumulation, but the real cost wasn't just in the hours spent packing and unpacking. It was the mental weight that came with it.

Stuff isn't free. Even after you've paid for it, it demands space, time, and attention. Every object holds a memory, a choice, or even an expectation, and whether you realize it or not, your brain is constantly processing it all.

It's not a myth — a clean space equals a clear mind.

You might think you're focused on your work, but in the background, your subconscious is scanning everything around you. That stack of unopened mail. The cluttered desk. A half-full coffee cup from this morning. Each item is a silent distraction, and sometimes, it's not so silent.

Imagine this: You're deep in work when your eyes catch a small souvenir from your trip to the Netherlands. Suddenly, a memory pops up — *"That trip was amazing. I loved that little French restaurant…"* Within moments, you've picked up your phone and opened a travel site. You're not planning a vacation; you're just reliving the past.

Now, two things have happened:

1. **Your focus is gone.** Productivity takes a hit as your mind drifts away.
2. **Your subconscious is working overtime.** Even if you don't act on the thought, your brain is replaying memories, reliving emotions, and processing regrets or longing.

That's the hidden cost of clutter and it's not just about physical space. It's emotional, mental, and even spiritual. The more things you have, the more mental tabs remain open — draining your energy without you even knowing it.

Why Do We Accumulate?

Every time I moved, I asked myself: *Why did I keep all this?* I only ever used a few plates, slept on one bed, and wore the same handful of clothes I actually liked. Yet I had closets bursting with things I didn't need, and I'm not alone.

Accumulation is often fueled by comparison and competition. It's easy to fall into the belief that more means better, but what I've learned is that whether you're wealthy or living on a budget, happiness doesn't come from excess. It comes from intentionality.

I'm not suggesting you reject nice things. Quite the opposite. Wanting quality is natural, and enjoying beautiful, well-made items is part of life, but the key is to want what serves you, what makes you happy, and what aligns with your life.

When we stop mindless consumption, something powerful happens. We shift the demand. Companies are forced to chase quality, not just churn out endless products, and when you buy with intention, even luxury becomes more meaningful, but regardless of your choices, quality over quantity should always be the goal.

How to Clear Your Space — And Your Mind

Decluttering isn't just about tidying up. It's about reclaiming your mental clarity. When your surroundings are clear, your brain has fewer distractions. Decision fatigue is reduced. Focus sharpens.

Here's how to start:

- **Start with your desk.** Keep only what you use daily. Remove unnecessary decor and distractions.
- **Declutter one room at a time.** Donate or discard items that no longer serve a purpose. Even clutter hidden in drawers can weigh on your mind.
- **Apply the "hotel rule."** Imagine walking into your home as if it were a luxury hotel room. Would you want to see tangled wires, piles of paper, or unused gadgets? Create a space that feels calm and intentional.
- **Digitally declutter.** Clean out old emails, uninstall unused apps, and organize your desktop. A messy digital space is just as draining as a cluttered room.
- **Be intentional with decor.** A single plant or a well-chosen painting can enhance your space without overwhelming it. Visual noise is mental noise.

Ever wonder why people return from vacations feeling mentally refreshed? It's not just the break from routine. It's the absence of visual clutter. Hotels don't display piles of old bills or half-finished projects.

Step 3B: Programming Your Brain for Fitness

Before you change your body, you need to **program your brain**.
At this point, you've spent a day alone in nature. You've decluttered your space.
You **know what you truly want.**
For most people, the **core goals** are pretty universal:

- Be **healthy**.
- Lose **weight** and get in **shape**.

- Achieve **financial freedom.**
- Have a **strong relationship** or find someone special.

And then there's that small group of us who secretly want to dominate the world. (Relax, just kidding... kind of.)

Whatever your goal is, **it all starts with programming.**

Let's repeat this part. If you constantly tell yourself, "I need to lose weight," your focus stays on the weight itself—reinforcing its presence in your mind. Instead, shift your perspective. Accept your body as it is today. Focus on what you like about it, and then, without obsessing over the outcome, simply commit to the steps that will shape the version of yourself you desire.

Don't dwell on the number on the scale. Instead, visualize the process—the workouts, the movement, the way your body feels as it gets stronger. See yourself already in your ideal shape. When you stop fixating on losing and start focusing on becoming, the transformation happens naturally.

Because your subconscious **is always working**—even when you're not. If you keep feeding it this idea, it will **start preparing for the transformation before you even take action.**

Think about this:

When you sleep, imagine your ideal body. See yourself strong, lean, and full of energy.

Visualize yourself doing workouts. Picture yourself making healthy food choices. Before you physically start exercising, mentally rehearse it.

- Imagine standing in *mountain pose*.
- See yourself transitioning into *downward dog*, then *upward dog*.
- Watch a couple of yoga videos—not to start immediately, but to let your **mind get used to the idea**.

Your **subconscious needs to create capacity first**—otherwise, you'll just be **forcing yourself** and eventually quitting.

The more your **brain prepares for something, the easier it becomes**.

Start Simple—Movement is Key. Once your mind is ready, it's time to move your body.

The rule? Keep it simple.

You do not need an extreme fitness program. You do not need to spend hours at the gym. The only thing that matters is that you move. Do what you enjoy. If you love running, run. If you love yoga, practice yoga. If you prefer strength training, do it.

Here's a **basic starting point**:

- **Walking** – The simplest, most underrated form of exercise. Walk **every single day**. No excuses.
- **Push-ups** – One of the best full-body movements. Start with 5. Work your way up.
- **A few yoga moves** – Just enough to activate your **metabolism** and improve **flexibility**.

When you're stuck in a long, boring cardio session, measuring time by songs instead of minutes can make it feel like it's flying by. Instead of staring at the clock, let the rhythm take over—tell yourself, just three more songs and suddenly, you're in the zone. "And, baby, I just can't get enough..." the music pulses through you, each beat pushing you forward, making every step feel a little less like work and a little more like surrendering to the moment.

These **small movements** trigger **big changes** in your body, and here's the thing—**once you start moving, your body will naturally want more.**

Daily movement improves health, but everyone's starting point is different.

Step 3C: Simplifying Your Diet

Stop Obsessing. Start Programming.

Once again, the more you obsess over your weight, looks, or workouts, the more you trap yourself in an endless loop of frustration. Stop micromanaging every bite of food. Stop chasing perfection. Stop feeling guilty for every missed workout.

Instead, **program your desires into your subconscious and put them on autopilot.**

Build a system. Set routines. Do the small things daily that move you forward.

One day, you'll wake up and realize—without even thinking about it—you've become the version of yourself you always wanted to be. **Stronger. Leaner. More confident. More powerful.**

Success isn't about obsessing over every step. It's about programming your mind and letting the process unfold.

Autopilot your growth. Let time do the work.

Food is Fuel—That's it.

Yes, food is fuel, but for many, it's also comfort, nostalgia, and a coping mechanism for stress, loneliness, or trauma. Understanding this is the first step to lasting weight loss. You are not weak or undisciplined if you struggle with food—it simply means your mind and body are working from outdated programming.

Weight loss is not just about food choices—it's about reprogramming your habits for long-term success. Before making changes, you must first prepare your mind. Jumping into a new diet without mental preparation is the biggest mistake people make. Instead, spend time visualizing your ideal relationship with food and structuring your eating habits. When your mind is ready, your body will follow.

Most weight loss failures stem from mental resistance, not just physical limitations. If you've tried diets before and failed, it wasn't because you lacked willpower—it was because the system you followed wasn't sustainable for you.

Try this first:

- **Visualize the Future You** – Every morning, picture yourself in your ideal body—how you feel, move, and exist in that version of yourself.
- **Speak Reality into Existence** – Stop saying, "I can't lose weight." Instead, say, "I am becoming leaner and stronger every day."
- **Remove Identity Blocks** – Saying, "I have a slow metabolism" reinforces the struggle. Instead, say, "I am learning how to fuel my body for energy and balance."
- **Acknowledge Emotional Eating Without Shame** – If food has been a comfort, don't punish yourself. Recognize that you are learning new coping mechanisms instead of relying on food.
- **Simplify Your Approach** – The more complicated a diet is, the harder it is to follow. Focus on nutrient-dense, whole foods and structured eating patterns.

Yes, weight loss at its core follows the rule:

Calories burned > Calories consumed = Fat loss

Your body is not a calculator—it's a system. Stress, hormones, gut health, and emotional well-being all play a role in whether weight comes off easily or stubbornly resists change.

Aligning mind and body begins with simple eating rules. Your body fights complexity—it was never designed to process dozens of ingredients and conflicting signals. The simpler your diet, the easier weight loss and overall balance become. Instead of obsessing over calories, macros, or numbers, focus on building a system that works *for you*—a rhythm of nourishment that your body understands and your mind can sustain with ease.

A Simple 1,500-Calorie Meal Plan (Adjust as Needed)

- **Breakfast:** Eggs + avocado (250 cal)
- **Lunch:** Grilled chicken + quinoa + veggies (500 cal)
- **Snack:** Greek yogurt + berries (200 cal)
- **Dinner:** Salmon + roasted vegetables (550 cal)

Vegans, of course, have their own alternatives to explore.

The Formula for a Sustainable Diet

- Protein + Healthy Fats + Greens
- One Consistent Eating Schedule

- Fasting (When You're Ready, Not Forced)

Why Fasting is Powerful—But Not for Everyone

Research by Nobel Prize-winning scientist Yoshinori Ohsumi has shown that fasting activates autophagy, a process where cells break down and recycle their own components. This helps:

- Reduce inflammation
- Optimize metabolism
- Prevent metabolic diseases

If you struggle with binge eating, emotional eating, or high stress, fasting can backfire. Instead, focus on structured meal timing first and gradually introduce fasting once your metabolism stabilizes.

Why Most Diets Fail

People chase new diets and workout trends because they're sold a fantasy—overnight transformation, but ask yourself:

How long did it take to gain the weight?

Was it a single meal or years of habits?

Weight gain happens gradually. Fat loss happens the same way—slow, consistent, disciplined.

Instead of "going on a diet," reprogram your identity:

- "I am someone who fuels my body with intention."
- "I am someone who moves daily."

- "I listen to my hunger cues and eat what truly nourishes me."

In your daily life, try to treat food as fuel, ensuring you get the nutrients your body needs to function optimally. However, from time to time, allow yourself to enjoy a special meal. If you can afford it, treat yourself to a nice restaurant—it's not just about eating but about creating an experience. Dining out offers an opportunity to step away from routine, enjoy something special, and even create romantic moments or social connections that enrich your life. Make time to enjoy great meals, explore different flavours, and dine out occasionally. A well-prepared meal can be a social, romantic, or cultural experience. Keep your daily diet structured, but allow space for enjoyment.

Step 3D: Refining Your Wardrobe

Do not underestimate the importance of fashion. **It is how you express yourself to the world, even to strangers, before you ever say a word.** The way you present yourself reflects confidence, self-respect, and even the way you approach life, **but don't get carried away.** It's easy to fall into the trap of chasing trends, accumulating unnecessary pieces, or believing that style is about excess rather than refinement. **True elegance comes from knowing what works for you, curating a wardrobe with intention, and wearing it with confidence.**

Invest in essential pieces. A well-thought-out wardrobe is not about having endless options—it's about having the **right** ones. A beautifully put-together outfit can lose its impact if it isn't paired with the right shoes. An outfit is nothing if not paired with the right pair of SHOES.

Wardrobe Must-Haves

A well-curated wardrobe isn't about excess—it's about quality, versatility, and timeless pieces that make you feel confident and effortlessly put together. These essentials work for any occasion, eliminating decision fatigue and ensuring you always look polished.

For Women

The Perfect Black Dress – A classic, go-to piece that transitions seamlessly from day to night.

A Comfortable Yet Stylish Sweat Suit – If you can, invest in a high-quality cashmere set for both luxury and comfort.

Flawless Black Trousers (or a Black Skirt, if preferred) – A well-tailored fit that pairs effortlessly with anything.

A Well-Fitted Black Blazer – Instantly elevates any outfit, whether paired with jeans or trousers.

Accessories That Highlight Your Features – Scarves, earrings, and statement pieces that enhance your natural beauty, especially your eyes.

A Pair of Perfect Sneakers – Comfortable, stylish, and suitable for everyday wear.

Well-Made Jeans – The ultimate staple—find a pair that fits flawlessly and lasts for years.

A Pair of Black Shoes – A classic square-heeled option that works equally well with skirts and trousers.

For Men

A Comfortable Yet Stylish Sweat Suit – Opt for a well-structured set in quality fabric.

Tailored Black Trousers – A staple for both professional and casual settings.

A Well-Fitted Black Blazer – Elevates any outfit, whether paired with dress pants or jeans.

A Crisp, High-Quality Shirt – Essential for both formal and semi-casual occasions.

A Pair of Perfect Sneakers – Comfortable and effortlessly stylish.

Well-Made Jeans – A properly fitted pair that balances casual and refined.

Classic Black Loafers – A must-have for any polished wardrobe.

Less is more. Invest in quality, choose timeless over trendy, and build a wardrobe that simplifies your life while keeping you effortlessly stylish.

Never sacrifice comfort—not in shoes, not in clothing, not in anything. Style and confidence come from how you carry yourself, and that's impossible when you're constantly adjusting an uncomfortable outfit or wincing with every step in painful shoes. **The best fashion choice is the one that makes you feel effortless.**

You don't need more clothes—you need a system.

Most people make clothing **more complicated than it needs to be.**

I used to overcomplicate clothing. If I bought this dress, it needed those shoes. If I bought these pants, they required that blazer. Every new piece seemed to demand another, creating an endless cycle of consumption. Then, due to some bad habits, and life's natural fluctuations, I gained weight—and suddenly, most of my closet became useless. What did that mean? Another shopping spree to replace it all.

I love fashion. I love the feeling of wearing a beautifully crafted sweater, perfectly tailored trousers, or an elegant dress. I grew up listening to my grandmother talk about the importance of fabric, stitching, colour, and shape. However, over time, I realized I could still have that feeling without making things so complicated.

So, I took a step back and carefully considered my lifestyle and routine. Some women are naturally great at this—curating a timeless, functional wardrobe. Others struggle. The same applies to men, though with fewer options, they often do a better job at keeping it simple.

The key is finding balance—building a wardrobe that works for you, not against you. Fashion should enhance your life, not create unnecessary stress.

People have a closet full of clothes, but **struggle to decide what to wear** because there's no structure, no theme, and no strategy.

Think of highly successful people—they often wear **the same type of outfit every day** because they've eliminated **decision fatigue**.

- **Steve Jobs** had his black turtleneck and jeans.
- **Barack Obama** rotated between just a few suit colours.
- **Mark Zuckerberg** sticks to grey T-shirts.

You don't need to go that extreme, but you **do** need a **defined personal style** that makes getting dressed **simple and effortless**.

How to Build a Functional, Stylish Wardrobe

- **Dress for your lifestyle.**

  If you work in an office, invest in **structured, high-quality basics**.

  If you work from home, keep things **comfortable but polished**—not just sweats.

  If you travel often, choose **wrinkle-resistant, easy-to-pack items**.

- **Dress for your body type.**

  Trends come and go. Focus on **what actually suits your frame**.

  Understand **cuts and fits** that flatter your shape and stick to them.

- **Dress for your colour theme.**

Colours influence **mood, confidence, and energy**.

Experiment with what makes you feel **powerful, calm, or focused**.

Create a **palette** that works for you—this makes shopping much easier.

- **Invest in a few high-quality essentials.**

  Instead of buying **cheap trendy clothes**, own **10 solid, high-quality pieces**.

  A **perfect blazer** is better than 10 ill-fitting jackets.

  A **well-made pair of shoes** will outlast several cheap ones.

- **Stick to your signature look.**

  Once you find a **formula that works**, don't overcomplicate it.

  If you love **white button-down shirts**, buy a few of the same style.

  If **black jeans fit perfectly**, replace them with the same model when they wear out.

- **Reinvent your style as your life evolves.**

  Every few years, **adjust your wardrobe** to match the direction of your life.

  New job? New phase in life? **Upgrade accordingly.**

- **Your hair is part of your style.**

- Coco Chanel (Une femme qui se coupe les cheveux est sur le point de changer de vie.) "A woman who cuts her hair is about to change her life." — Your hairstyle is the **first thing you visualize** when imagining a **new version of yourself**.

  Changing your hair is often the **first physical step** in **reinventing yourself**.

Final Thoughts.

Think of your brain as a computer:

- Old habits? Outdated software.
- Negative self-talk? Viruses slowing your system.
- Complicated diets? Unnecessary apps consuming RAM.

Start simple:

Walk. Do push-ups. Practice yoga. Movement is the priority. Eat real food on a consistent schedule. Fast. It's not a restriction—it's a way to let your body function properly.

Overcomplicating food choices leads to failure. Simplicity and listening to your body lead to success. There are no shortcuts. Real change happens the same way weight gain did—slowly, consistently, and with discipline. The key isn't the latest "miracle" diet. It's building a sustainable system that works for you. First, program your brain. Your subconscious needs to prepare before your body does.

Present yourself as the best version of **you**.

- Style should simplify, not complicate.
- Choose quality over quantity.
- From time to time, reinvent yourself—keep life exciting.

When you simplify fitness, diet, and your wardrobe, you eliminate:

- Stress
- Overthinking
- Unnecessary spending
- The cycle of starting and quitting

Mastering your body and mind lays the foundation for everything else in life. The habits you cultivate and the level of self-respect you maintain will shape the relationships you build. You cannot expect from others what you haven't first built within yourself.

Step 4: Relationships & Finding the Right Partner

While many principles of *relationship-building* are universal, some suggestions or recommendations may be overlooked simply because they stem from a heterosexual perspective. That being said, the core values of *respect, communication, attraction, and personal growth* apply to all relationships, regardless of their structure.

"A relationship is like a road trip. You better pick the right person to be in the car with, or you'll spend the whole journey arguing over directions."

Do not underestimate your abilities. We are all unique. If you ever doubt that, just look at your **fingerprints**—no two people have the same ones. That is not a coincidence.
Whether you believe in **God, the universe, fate, or science**, the message is the same:
You are here to leave **your** mark on the world. So stop trying to **be someone else**. Stop trying to **compete with someone else's life**. Competition is healthy—it pushes us forward—but the **only real competition that matters is with yourself**.
Be better than **you were yesterday**. Every single day.

Don't wait until you're **60 or 70** to realize that your **mindset is finally in the right place, but your body didn't keep up.** Don't wait until you have **financial freedom** but **no one to share it with.**

That image you have in your head—of you, somewhere beautiful, with comoone you love, feeling completely happy?

Build the habits now to make that a reality.

Yes, we all make mistakes.

"Only a fool learns from his own mistakes. The wise man learns from the mistakes of others." Otto von Bismarck

So why not learn from my mistakes? **Why not live life like a wise man?**

Cleaning your space, organizing your wardrobe, creating your personal system— these were important steps, but now we move to something even more crucial: Relationships.

Yes, you heard me. Before we talk about **money**, we talk about **love.**

Because **money should be a tool to support your life, not the reason you live it.**

We Are Meant to Be With Someone

I didn't have to look far to believe in good men. I was raised around them.

My father, my uncles—they were the embodiment of what real masculinity looks like when it's done right. Not the loud, aggressive kind that tries to control everything. The quiet, confident kind. The kind that listens before speaking, laughs often, shows up, and stays.

They were strong, yes—but not just in the way they carried weight or worked with their hands. They were strong in patience, in emotional presence, in the way they made space for others. They loved their partners openly, without games. They were evolving, emotionally intelligent, even romantic—and yes, somehow still good-looking while fixing broken things around the house or dancing in the kitchen without rhythm.

From them, I learned that it's entirely possible to find a man who is both grounded and wild. Someone who brings humor into the hard moments, who doesn't run from chaos but holds you through it. They were confident but never arrogant, playful but never careless, dependable without being dull.

Growing up around that kind of love shaped my standards without me even realizing it. I saw what it looked like when a man didn't just follow the rules of love, but created his own—tailored to the woman he adored. The love I witnessed was built on small, consistent moments that were anything but ordinary: the silent teamwork over morning coffee, the shared glances across crowded rooms, the steady hand on the back when words weren't needed.

It was steady and wild. Structured and spontaneous. Strong, but never hard.

And because I saw it—I know it's possible.

Nothing can derail your life quite like a bad marriage, and more often than not, a bad marriage isn't about having a bad spouse—it's about having a partner whose values, goals, and outlook on life don't align with yours. Differences in culture, upbringing, education, or ambitions can create a disconnect that's impossible to bridge.

A mismatched marriage won't just make you unhappy—it will hold you back. If you were meant to fly, it will clip your wings. It will drain your energy, dull your potential, and leave you feeling stuck in a life that doesn't feel like your own.

That being said, life is far more enjoyable when shared. Experiences, travels, challenges, growth—it's all better with the right person by your side, but let's be clear: **if you're in the wrong relationship, it's better to be alone.**

In the BBC series *Sherlock*, Sherlock Holmes asserts, 'Alone is what I have. Alone protects me.' While I know this is taken out of context, there are moments when it rings true. Sometimes, being alone is better than staying with someone who repeatedly and intentionally causes you pain.

A good relationship is:

- Accepting—not judgmental.
- Supportive—not competitive.
- Loving—not manipulative.

It's not about control, power, or keeping score.

And here's the simplest test: **if you see your partner in a crowd and your heart doesn't skip a beat, you're in the wrong relationship.**

The Heart Test

Love isn't complicated. It's not supposed to be.

It's not a checklist. It's not a dating profile.

It's a feeling — and your body always knows before your mind does.

Your heart should skip a beat. That's not just a romantic cliché — it's *real*.

Studies have shown that when you're in love, your heart rate can literally change in response to the person you're with. Your body responds before you can explain why. Your breathing shifts. Your heartbeat accelerates or syncs with theirs. You feel energized… and calm. Safe… but excited. You smile without thinking. That's chemistry. That's alignment. That's the kind of love worth building a life on. We've been conditioned to overthink relationships — to strategize, to settle, to make it work even when it clearly doesn't, but if your heart doesn't react — if it doesn't skip, if it doesn't stir — then it's not *that* kind of love. It's comfort. Or obligation. Or fear of being alone.

And you deserve more than that. **True love should move you. Physically. Emotionally. Spiritually.** You don't need a spreadsheet of pros and cons. You need one moment of truth — one skipped heartbeat. That's your compass.

A real partnership is built on true love and requires:

- **Shared goals** – Do you both want a simple, healthy lifestyle, or are you constantly clashing?
- **Aligned expectations** – Are you both striving for long-term success, stability, and fulfillment?
- **Mutual attraction and admiration** – Do you take pride in each other's growth, health, and efforts?

The best relationships allow both partners to evolve into the best version of themselves. If you feel restricted, drained, or uninspired, it's not the right one.

Now, take a couple whose values align:

- They both prioritize health and fitness.
- They actively support each other's growth.

- They take personal pride in one another's accomplishments, looks, and well-being.
- They share undeniable physical chemistry.

That's an unbreakable bond.

It's not about luck. It's about **choosing correctly**—and putting in the effort to maintain it.

The concept of **yin and yang** dates back thousands of years to ancient Chinese philosophy. It describes how seemingly opposite forces—light and dark, masculine and feminine, active and receptive—are actually interconnected and interdependent. Each one contains a seed of the other, and together, they create balance and harmony in the universe. What's often misunderstood is that **yin and yang aren't halves—they are wholes.** Each is already a complete and powerful energy on its own. But when they come together, something even more profound happens. Like two intricate puzzle pieces or mirrored images, they form a single, unified symbol—not by losing themselves, but by complementing and completing each other. In the same way, a perfect relationship isn't about finding your "missing half." It's about two whole beings, each grounded in their essence, choosing to align. Together, they don't just make sense—they create harmony.

Love thrives on exclusivity, respect, and genuine connection. If you're easily swayed by fleeting looks or triggered by vanity, you're not ready for a mature relationship. Insecurity takes the lead, and before long, it turns love into a battlefield of unspoken fears and projected doubts.

True love builds — it never belittles.

When someone is genuinely confident — in their appearance, their worth, and their intellect — they're also confident in their choice. They don't crave the approval of strangers. Their validation comes from within, and from the one person they've

chosen to share their heart with. In that kind of confidence, loyalty isn't a struggle —
it's second nature.

Men

A Thought for Men

Let's have an honest conversation.

For centuries, stories have shown us the importance of making choices with integrity
and purpose. Acting on impulse without accountability can lead to regret — not only
for yourself but also for those around you. Building character means making
conscious decisions, being proud of the path you choose, and committing to
something greater than fleeting desires.

In today's world, distractions are everywhere — social media, endless comparisons,
and the constant allure of instant gratification. It's easy to get caught up in the chase
for validation, but relationships deserve more than that. If you don't see a meaningful
future with your partner, it's okay to let go. Staying out of fear of loneliness or
comfort serves neither of you. Moving on with honesty and respect is not a failure —
it's a reflection of growth and self-awareness.

True strength lies in self-control, discipline, and acting with intention. It's not about
suppressing feelings but about leading with your heart and mind, not just your
instincts. Relationships thrive on mutual respect, understanding, and effort. Both
partners should feel supported, valued, and empowered to grow. If you or your
partner are unwilling to grow together, it may be time to reevaluate.

If commitment isn't something you're ready for, be upfront. Embrace your freedom and explore your desires — but be mindful of others' intentions. Respect your partner's time, emotions, and hopes. Everyone deserves clarity and honesty.

And when you do choose someone, choose them fully. A healthy relationship means your partner knows where they stand, without uncertainty. Show your dedication by being present, appreciating them, and continuously supporting their growth. Love isn't sustained by attraction alone; it deepens through kindness, effort, and shared commitment.

Before making a decision, pause and reflect: Are your actions aligned with the person you want to become? Growth is always possible, and every choice is a chance to become a better version of yourself.

Be proud of the man you are — and the one you're becoming.

Women

Women, This Goes for You Too

The same rules apply.
Be **proud of your choice**.
Stop manipulating situations to always get your way. Stop using **emotions as a tool for power**. If you need to constantly test, manipulate, or "train" your partner, then you're with the wrong person. The **right relationship** doesn't need games.
It's completely understandable that relationships take time to reveal their true nature. In the beginning, it's natural to question whether a partnership will grow into a strong, supportive bond — one built on mutual love, respect, and shared growth, but

sometimes, there comes a moment of clarity when you realize that no matter how much effort you pour in, the teamwork you hoped for will never materialize. If you're not receiving the support, love, and care you deserve — and if you're unable to give the same in return — it's not a partnership; it's a slow unraveling of yourself. In those moments, honesty is the most courageous choice you can make. Walk away. It will hurt, and the healing will take time, but it's far better to face that temporary pain than to lose yourself piece by piece in a relationship that no longer serves your growth. Letting go isn't failure — it's self-respect, and in time, you'll find that the space you create by leaving will make room for something healthier, something that feels like home.

Lilith: The Woman Who Refused to Settle

Long before Eve, there was Lilith.

You don't often hear her story—but in the oldest versions, whispered between ancient lines and tucked into forgotten folklore, Lilith was the first woman. Not made from Adam's rib, but formed from the very same earth. Equal. Not a part of him—his counterpart, his mirror.

They were together for a time. But when Adam demanded obedience—when he expected her to bow simply because he was a man—Lilith didn't shrink. She didn't argue. She didn't make herself smaller to keep the peace.

She left.

In one final, defiant act, she spoke the secret name of God—a name so powerful it unlocked the gates of Eden. And she walked away. Away from comfort, away from certainty, away from a man who couldn't see her as his equal. Later, they called her a demon. But often, that's what history becomes when a woman dares to write her own version of it.

Then came Eve—crafted not from earth, but from Adam's rib. She was everything Adam wanted: soft, compliant, designed to fit. She was created not to challenge him, but to complete him. That detail alone says everything.

Lilith's story was never about wickedness. It was about boundaries. About knowing your worth—even when it costs you everything. It was about choosing freedom over approval. Self-respect over comfort.

The lesson? Don't become someone's rib when you were born of the same earth.

If you want real love, don't look for someone to complete you. Look for someone who already sees you as whole. Because here's the truth: sometimes one person simply isn't ready for growth. When that happens, they may label their partner as "difficult"—not because the partner is unreasonable, but because growth requires effort. And not everyone is willing to rise. If someone calls you too much, too intense, or too demanding—pause. Often, it's not a reflection of who you are, but of the standards they are unwilling or unable to meet. The right partner won't see your strength as a threat. They'll see it as an invitation—to grow, to evolve, to become better. Stay rooted in your values. Don't dilute them to keep someone who isn't evolving beside you.

In a relationship built on trust and respect, jealousy has no place. Imagine being in a room full of distractions—wandering eyes, fleeting interest, temptation. But you're calm. Confident. Present. Because when love is secure, it doesn't compete. It just is.

A woman who knows she is valued has no need to fear comparison. Because the connection she holds isn't fragile—it's deeply rooted. No glance, no flirtation, no passing thrill can shake the ground you've built together.

In a 2015 interview at Fortune's Most Powerful Women Summit, Warren Buffett joked, "If you want a marriage to last, look for someone with low expectations." While likely meant in jest, it touches on a deeper truth: lower expectations reduce conflict— but they also reduce growth.

Lasting love isn't built on resignation. It's built on challenge. On mutual ambition. On two people choosing to rise—together.

Unfortunately, many settle for comfort. They choose partners who require little, expect little, challenge little—because it feels easier. But there is nothing fulfilling about shrinking yourself to maintain peace.

The most powerful relationships are not the easiest—they're the ones that demand your highest self. The ones where both people are willing to stretch, evolve, and meet each other fully. These relationships aren't just routines. They're legacies.

Because true love doesn't ask you to stay the same—it invites you to become more.

A relationship rooted in growth is not about someone who simply accepts your flaws. It's about someone who sees your potential and pushes you toward it. Who celebrates your ambition and stands beside you as you step into the next version of yourself.

Settling for less in love is settling for less in life.

Expect more—from your relationship, from your partner, and most importantly, from yourself.

And that brings us to something deeper.

For much of human history, women were not active in the workforce—not because they lacked intelligence or potential, but because their biological systems played a key role in preserving emotional and generational balance. The female body is finely tuned to stress, safety, and connection—designed not just for survival, but for continuity and healing.

This was never about limitation. It was about protection. And for a time, I believe a balance existed—where women could honour their nature without being confined by it. Where contribution and wellbeing could coexist.

But over centuries, that balance was lost. What may have begun as reverence became restriction. Women were not only protected—they were silenced. Their roles were narrowed, their voices suppressed, their power feared.

And now, we're on the other extreme.

Women are expected to do it all—to lead, to nurture, to achieve, to provide. The progress we've made is worth celebrating, and I would never suggest we undo it. But in the pursuit of "more," we've neglected something essential: balance.

We've learned to value productivity over presence. Achievement over alignment. We've glorified burnout as a badge of honour.

But the body doesn't lie.

When a woman feels emotionally safe and fully seen—regardless of gender dynamics—her entire system responds. Cortisol lowers. Oxytocin and serotonin rise. Her nervous system softens. Over time, this creates true hormonal balance, emotional steadiness, and lasting vitality.

These are not abstract ideas. They are biological truths.

This is not a call to go backwards. It's a call to move forward with consciousness. To build a world where feminine energy isn't overextended or overlooked—but honoured. Where strength includes softness. Where doing is balanced by being.

Though I speak from my own experience—as a woman in a heterosexual relationship—the core truth applies to all: every human deserves to feel safe, valued, and fully seen. Because when we are, we thrive. Not through force. Not through compromise. But through harmony.

That's the path forward.

Money & Relationships

Money is a tool to support your life goals.

It is **not**:

- A way to **control your partner**.
- A way to **compete** with your partner.
- A **power move** to have an upper hand in the relationship.

If **either person** in the relationship is using money as leverage, the foundation is already broken.

A strong relationship is built on:

- Mutual respect.
- Shared ambition.
- A common vision for life.

Sometimes, circumstances won't be equal—one person's career or personal growth may take precedence for a time. **That doesn't mean the power dynamic should shift.** Marriage is a team effort. If one partner has a better opportunity to grow at the moment, the focus should be on supporting that path, but that support should never come at the expense of the other's dreams.

Success is cyclical. **One person may lead today, but tomorrow, the roles could reverse.** The key is to never let temporary circumstances define permanent dynamics. A strong relationship ensures that **both partners feel seen, valued, and empowered to pursue their own ambitions.**

The Relationship You Want Starts With YOU. Everything **starts within.**
If you are **not happy with yourself,** you will **never be happy with someone else.**
Go back to the first chapters:
- Have you **optimized your body?**
- Have you **cleaned your space?**
- Have you **found clarity in what you truly want?**
Once you're in a relationship, the **real work begins.**
- Be **sexy.**

- Be **smart**.
- Be **interesting**.
- Be **engaging**.
- Bring **love, creativity, care, and sexiness** into the relationship.

Because if you don't?

Every relationship will end up the same.

Boring sex. Boring conversations.

Let's be clear—love and physical connection matter. Hugs, cuddles, closeness—they're not extras; they're essential. You need to create an atmosphere where these things happen naturally, without pressure or obligation. There is nothing more liberating, more grounding, than intimacy with your partner—where mind and body align effortlessly. In that space, love isn't just felt—it's embodied. Connection becomes instinctive.

However it can only happen when there are:

- No **anger and resentment** building up.
- No **expectations or silent punishments**.
- No **manipulation or games**.

Entering Relationships with a Clean Slate

By the time you reach the stage in life where you are choosing a **partner**, you are **already carrying baggage**.

You've been hurt. You've been let down.

Maybe you've been cheated on, or perhaps **you were the one who took someone for granted**, only to watch them walk away.

Maybe you **flirted too much** and lost someone special. Maybe you never **fully moved on** from a past love, secretly keeping track of that person, hoping that one day, **destiny will bring you back together.**

No matter **what your past looks like**, when entering a new relationship, you have **one responsibility**:

- Get to know the person in front of you for who they truly are.
- Ask yourself honestly: Are there enough qualities you admire in this person?
- Can you truly see a future together?
- And most importantly: **give them a clean slate.**

- Do not punish them for your past relationships.
- Do not **disrespect them just because someone else once disrespected you.**
- Do not **take them for granted just because your last relationship allowed it.**

Instead, build a relationship that—no matter how it ends—you can look back on with peace and say:

"I gave my best. I loved deeply. I treated them with respect."

Let every relationship be a rebirth. A chance to show up as the best version of yourself—not perfect, but present, intentional, and whole.

Love, like music and dance, is more than words or actions. It's energy. It's rhythm. It's movement. When you're in sync with someone, you don't need to force or explain—it flows. The same way a song moves your body without thought, real love moves your soul without effort. And when it's done right, even the silence between you feels like harmony.

One of the simplest, most powerful ways to reignite that energy — in a relationship or within yourself — is through music and dance. Don't be afraid to be a foolish romantic. Dance. Be spontaneous. Laugh. Play music.

Too many people grow old not from age, but because they stop moving, stop feeling, and lose the music from their lives. Every culture has traditional dances for a reason. Music is woven into our history — a language of joy, sorrow, and celebration.

Be mindful of what you listen to. Our ancestors used music to prepare for war, celebrate weddings, mourn losses, and mark life's milestones. Now, research shows it can calm the nervous system, rewire the brain, and sharpen focus. We even have apps designed to simulate what's already instinctive — the power of sound to soothe, energize, or heal, but you don't need an app to bring music back. Dance like no one's watching. Feel the rhythm. Let it move through you. It can be a workout, a therapist, or a release — all in one.

If music has slipped away from your life, find it again.
For yourself.
For your relationships.
For your love life.

Because when words fail, when stress takes over, and emotions run high — music and dance can reset everything.

Pride Has No Place in Love and Marriage

Pride is useful in many areas of life—our careers, our personal achievements, our ability to stand tall in the face of challenges. However, in love, especially in marriage, pride can be a silent killer. It builds walls where there should be bridges. It creates distance where there should be closeness.

A happy, thriving relationship is built on **humility, kindness, and consistent effort**. When pride takes over, it stops us from doing the very things that nurture love— apologizing first, admitting when we're wrong, or making the first move to reconnect after an argument. Love should never be about *winning*—it's about growing together, about choosing each other over and over again.

The truth is, **most of us are just average people**. We haven't built the next spaceship that's going to Mars. We haven't solved the world's water crisis or discovered a new element. Yet somehow, we convince ourselves that we're too busy, too overwhelmed, too preoccupied to do something as simple as **love**.

We can't stop our minds from running in vicious circles about work stress, financial worries, or minor inconveniences, but we hesitate to send a kind word, give a heartfelt compliment, or show a little extra patience. Why? Because we take love for granted. We assume it will always be there, even if we stop nurturing it, but love, like anything meaningful, requires care and **deliberate effort**.

How Is It Fair?

How is it fair that out of pride, you refused to change?

You resisted being loving, refused to evolve — not because you couldn't, but because you wouldn't. And then, when it was too late, when they were gone, something shifted.

Suddenly, every truth they spoke, every mirror they held up, it all makes sense. Everything you resisted, every piece of wisdom you dismissed — now, you carry it. You move on, and this time, you're ready.
Ready to listen, to compromise, to be the version of yourself they once pleaded for.

And yet, the one who inspired that growth is no longer by your side.

It's a cruel irony — to become a better person because of them, but not *with* them. And as you build this new chapter, echoes of the past remain.
You can't help but wonder — do they know? Would they be proud of the person you've become?

And often, this reflection weaves into your present, because the heart doesn't forget. It aches not just for the loss, but for the wasted moments — the ones where love could have been louder than pride.

How is it fair?

The answer is — it's not.

Small Gestures, Big Impact

In the beginning of a relationship, effort comes naturally. Compliments flow easily. Thoughtful texts, surprises, and little gestures feel effortless. However, over time, as comfort sets in, these things start to fade. And when they do, the spark fades too.

The truth is, **romance doesn't die—it's neglected.** Keeping love alive doesn't require extravagant gestures. It's the small, **consistent** moments that keep relationships strong.

Here's how:

- **Send a note or message, just because.** A quick text saying, *I love you because...* or *I was just thinking about how much I appreciate you* can completely shift the energy of a relationship.
- **Compliment them often.** Not just when they dress up or on special occasions—acknowledge the little things. *I love how you laugh at your own jokes. I love the way you care for others.* People long to feel seen.
- **Share something personal.** Heard a song on the way to work that reminded you of them? Send it. Thought of a memory from your early days together? Bring it up. These small actions show that they are **always on your mind.**
- **Practice patience.** It's easy to snap when stressed, but real love is choosing patience over irritation, understanding over assumption, kindness over pride.

Love is a Program — Keep It Running

Love, like everything else in life, is a program. Think of it like an app you once downloaded — it was exciting, new, and full of possibilities, but over time, updates appear. If you never install them, the app becomes glitchy, outdated, and eventually loses its appeal. The same happens with love. If you don't make the effort to renew and nurture it, it won't remain as vibrant and exhilarating as it once was.

Love isn't something that just happens — it's something you create every day. The happiest couples aren't the ones who simply "got lucky" or found the perfect match. They are the ones who consistently choose each other, who make space for love amidst the noise of daily life. They keep showing up, learning, and growing together.

We pour energy into our jobs, deadlines, and endless distractions. What about love? If we can find time to stress and overthink, we can find time to appreciate and connect. Love isn't something that fades overnight — it fades slowly when we stop feeding it, but just as easily, it can be reignited.

Pause. Remember the beginning — the day you met, the moments that made your heart race, the reasons you couldn't wait to see them again. What made them stand out? What pulled you closer? That spark didn't disappear; it simply needs attention.

Like any program, love requires updates. Make time to create new memories. Notice the little things. See your partner not through the lens of familiarity, but through the eyes of the person who first fell in love with them. When you choose to nurture that connection, you'll find that love doesn't just survive — it thrives.

Pride has no place in love, but effort always does. Keep choosing your partner. Every single day.

Julius Caesar — a man of untamed power, who bent the course of history with his will alone. Armies bowed before him, cities crumbled at his command. He could have had anyone. The halls of Rome were lined with noblewomen longing for his favor, and yet, his gaze did not wander. His heart knew no hunger for fleeting desire.

For Caesar, love was not a conquest to be won or a game to be played. When he chose, it was with unwavering certainty. One woman. One devotion. In a world where indulgence was a birthright, he denied himself the easy pleasures that power could offer. His loyalty was a rare and dangerous thing — not given lightly, and never betrayed. Though temptation danced on gilded floors and whispered from darkened chambers, Caesar's eyes did not stray. He was a man who understood that strength was not in possessing many, but in choosing one — and holding fast. His name lives on, not only as a ruler who shaped empires, but as a man who, amidst the spoils of power, knew the truest victory was to love without question.

There's a reason I've spent so much time talking about love — because without it, we're little more than machines, moving through life on autopilot. Real love, the kind that brings companionship and true partnership, has the power to transform. It can turn the ordinary into the extraordinary, igniting brilliance where there was once only routine. In the right hands, even a simple soul can rise to greatness — not because love completes us, but because it awakens what was always there, waiting to be seen.

Final Thoughts on Relationships

Find the right person, or stay single.

Mutual values, goals, and attraction make a relationship last.

Men: Be fully consumed by the woman you choose—or don't choose at all.

Women: Be proud of your choice. Don't manipulate to get your way.

Money is a tool, not a power move.

Your happiness starts within. If you're not happy alone, you won't be happy together.

Keep the relationship alive—bring effort, creativity, and passion.

The healthiest relationships allow both partners to evolve into their best selves.

Find your music again

Love is not enough. You have to nurture it.

Love should feel like fire wrapped in calm—a balance of deep respect and wild desire. It should ground you and excite you all at once, pulling you into something bigger than just the moment. If you're going to share your energy with someone, make it unforgettable. Don't settle for comfort, convenience, or lukewarm connection. Hold out for the kind of love that makes your heart race, your body melt, and your soul feel seen. Once you've tasted that, nothing ordinary will ever satisfy you again.

Love is Wholehearted

Love is wholehearted, or it is nothing at all.

Not a whisper, not a shadow, not a fleeting call.

It does not come in halves, nor in careful disguise,

It consumes, it burns, it reaches the skies.

Love is not stagnant; it moves like the sea,

It bends, it sways, it longs to be free.

Yet in its freedom, it chooses to stay,

To grow, to deepen, never to stray.

To love and betray—such a hollow deceit,

To promise and wander is love's own defeat.

For love is a bond, a vow, a flame,

Not a fleeting thrill, not a careless game.

If you dishonour the one by your side,

You dishonour yourself, your soul, your pride.

For in choosing them, you chose a way,

A path, a promise, not just for today.

Only the weak seek glances anew,

Mistaking vanity for something true.

We are not creatures enslaved by desire,

Love is devotion, not fleeting fire.

A fortress must stand, or it is no home,

A love without roots is destined to roam.

If hands do not shield, if hearts do not fight,

Then love is a whisper, fading from sight.

Right or wrong, stand side by side,

Not with blind eyes, but arms open wide.

Correct with kindness, guide with grace,

But never let love lose its place.

For when values diverge, when passions fade,

Love turns to duty, then duty decays.

A life half-lived, a spark grown cold,

A story of love that was never bold.

But love is a fire, fierce and bright,

A beacon that cuts through the darkest night.

It does not wander, it does not wane,

It does not falter, it does not feign.

To love is to build, to shield, to stay,

To wake and choose them, day after day.

Not out of habit, nor out of need,

But because in their presence, your soul is freed.

Anna I

The Concept of Time

Marriage isn't just about the moment you say 'I do'—it's about the years, the decades, and the lifetime ahead. Love is felt in fleeting moments, but measured over time. It's time that tests love, strengthens it, or reveals its cracks. Whether it's a short-lived romance or a lifelong partnership, time has a way of uncovering what is real. Beyond relationships, time governs everything we do—our choices, our priorities, and ultimately, the life we build. What exactly is time, and how does understanding it change the way we live?

Have you ever watched a sand clock? Not just glanced at it, but really **watched it work**?

There are two profound lessons hidden in that slow cascade of falling grains.

First, **everything in life is built in small particles**. Nothing happens all at once. Every great achievement, every transformation, every journey—**they all begin with a single grain of effort, a single moment, a single choice.**

Second, **time is both fleeting and infinite**—it stretches or contracts depending on how you perceive it. If you sit and watch a single grain of sand fall, a minute feels like an eternity.

I have always been **one of the least patient people I know**. A close friend of mine used to tell me over and over, *"Patience is a virtue."* And as much as I hated hearing it, I eventually realized **it was true.**

But what is **patience**, really?

Patience is not just the ability to wait. **It is a calm state of mind—one that remains focused on the task at hand while allowing the subconscious mind to find solutions.** Patience is not about idly standing by, but about trusting that progress is being made, even if you can't always see it.

Society teaches us to obsess over time—to watch the clock, to measure minutes, to feel guilty for "wasting" time. Schedules dictate our lives, deadlines loom over us, and every second feels like it must be accounted for. But here's the truth: you should not constrain yourself to the rigid structure of time. Instead, *use time as a tool, not a cage.* That does not mean time isn't important. Of course, we have obligations, deadlines, and responsibilities. However, before you allow time to control you, **first understand how long each action truly takes.**

There are things we **all** must do, no matter who we are—whether rich or poor, powerful or unknown. These tasks are unavoidable, yet most people **never take the time to actually measure them.**

How long does it take for you to sleep well? Your body has an internal clock, but if it's misaligned, you need to **force a reset**. Wake up early and immediately **expose yourself to sunlight**—this signals your body to synchronize with the day.

How long does it take to shower, to cook, to eat? We do these things every day, yet we rarely analyze them.

Track these small, **inevitable** things. Know their rhythm, **then delegate that knowledge to your subconscious mind.**

For the next several weeks, **train yourself to mentally catalog** the time it takes to do everyday things. Not with stress, not with urgency—but simply **with awareness**.

Before you go to sleep each night, mentally **walk through your next day**:

- What will you do?
- What are the **non-negotiables**?
- What do you want to achieve?

Don't over-promise yourself and under-deliver. Instead, **come up with a simple step-by-step flow** and let your **subconscious handle the rest**.

Think about it. You are not actively thinking, *I need to breathe. I need to digest food. I need to blink.* These things happen on autopilot.

The goal is to delegate as many tasks as possible to your subconscious mind, freeing up mental space for what truly matters.

Once you master this, time **stretches**. You will fit more into one minute than you ever thought possible. You will move through life **fluidly, efficiently, effortlessly**—because time will no longer be something you chase. **It will be something you command.**

Reprogramming Yourself: The Balance Between Automation and Being Fully Alive

I keep coming back to this idea—that a **human can operate like a machine, like a computer**. And it's true. The way our **minds function**, the way our **habits shape us**, and the way **patterns define our lives**—all of it mirrors the logic of a system running on code, but don't mistake that for **one second** as me saying that we **are** machines.

We are **complex beings**—far beyond artificial intelligence, beyond cold logic. **We are driven by emotions, desires, love, and purpose.** What makes life **worth living** isn't efficiency. It's passion. It's the **messy, unpredictable beauty of being human.**

What you need to do is **separate the mundane from the life worth living**

Let the things that **don't require emotion**—the repetitive tasks, the daily habits, the essential but uninspiring parts of life—be handled on **autopilot.** Let your **subconscious take over**, so your **conscious mind is free for the things that truly matter.**

You are **not a robot.** You are **not an AI-enhanced machine.** You are a **human being,** and your energy should be spent **bringing back what makes life extraordinary:**

- **Bringing back romance**—Not just in relationships, but in how you see the world.
- **Taking joy in small moments**—A beautiful meal, a sunrise, a handwritten note.
- **Building, creating, loving, giving, nurturing**—The things that leave a real mark.

There is an Armenian poet **Yeghishe Charents** saying:

"Մահկանացու է մարդը, բայց անմահ է նրա գործը:"

Translated to English:

"Mortal is man, but immortal is his work."

Every single person has the opportunity to be **the best version of themselves.** However, by the time you reach your teenage years, it's already **difficult**—because you've been **programmed** by your upbringing.

Depending on the household you grew up in, you might already be conditioned to believe that **money is the only thing that matters**, that **love is everything**, or that **you need to struggle to survive.**

Maybe you were raised to **chase success at all costs**. Maybe you were raised to **sacrifice yourself for others**.

But here's the truth:

You can wipe your hard drive and reprogram your life.

You don't have to be **a slave to your past programming**.

You can **reset yourself to factory settings**, clear out the noise, and decide—**consciously, intentionally**—who you want to be.

Because in today's world, there are **no excuses**. You have **unlimited access to knowledge**. You can learn **anything, fix anything, rebuild anything**.

So why not use it to your **advantage**?

Why not **reprogram yourself into the best possible version of you?**

- **Stop** blaming.
- **Stop** finding excuses.
- **STOP**

You **have control** over your fate.

You **have control** over your life.

Take it back.

Step 5: Having Kids & Building Families

In all my life, I've never met someone who said they wanted to raise a truly evolved human being — someone emotionally strong, creative, independent, and ahead of their time. Most people don't set out to raise a superhuman; they simply follow the pattern. But imagine if we parented with that kind of intention — not just to have children, but to shape future leaders, healers, and visionaries.

Parenthood is Not a Fairytale. There is an old Armenian folk tale about a young mother who, cradling her newborn son, went to seek wisdom from the village's wisest elder. With hope in her eyes, she asked, "Please, teach me how to raise my son to be the smartest he can be." The old man looked at the child, then at the mother, and sighed. "It is already too late," he said. "You should have come to me before he was born." At first, the mother was confused. How could it be too late when the child's life had only just begun? However, as the elder explained, she came to understand a truth as old as time itself—long before a child takes his first breath, before he even enters the world, his journey has already begun. A mother's thoughts, emotions, and well-being shape the life growing within her. The way she nurtures herself—physically, mentally, and spiritually—becomes the foundation upon which her child will stand. Every feeling she experiences, every bite she eats, every fear or joy she carries in her heart—these, too, are passed down. This tale is a reminder that a mother's responsibility begins long before birth. It is not only about guiding a child after they arrive, but about shaping the world they enter. Women are the first architects of human potential, and the care they take in their own lives ripples into the lives of the generations that follow.

While not every path to parenthood looks the same—whether through surrogacy, adoption, or other means—the energy, intention, and love we bring into a child's life still carry profound influence.

Big families can be a beautiful thing, but only if you're fully prepared to give each child the love, attention, and support they deserve—if you're certain you won't unintentionally neglect the younger ones, then go for it.

The world is **not** suffering from a lack of people. If anything, it is **overflowing**. This planet is barely surviving under the weight of **pollution, waste, and mindless consumerism**. Humanity is expanding, yet **true human values** seem to be shrinking. If you are going to **bring children into this world**, do it **with purpose**. Make the effort to **raise them into well-rounded, healthy, accomplished individuals**—human beings who are **capable, strong, and ready to leave a meaningful imprint on this world**. Otherwise, **don't do it**.

Do not have children because it is **expected of you**.

Society tells you to **get married, have kids, and continue the cycle**, but **this is your life**, and you should not be **mindlessly repeating patterns** just because everyone else is doing it.

Forget the **Social Media version of parenting**—the glamorous, romanticized pregnancy photos, the glowing mothers with perfect hair, the artistic baby announcements.

That's **not** reality.

Reality is **sleepless nights**.

Reality is **constant worries, fears, and financial obligations**.

Reality is **an all-consuming responsibility that never truly goes away**.

If you are **not ready to do it right, do not commit**.

The Right Way to Raise Children

If you've followed the steps above, you'll have built a structured life — one that opens up space for what truly matters. You'll have the time to play with your child, understand their unique personality, and recognize both their strengths and the areas where they need support. In that space, you'll not only nurture their growth but also deepen the bond you share, shaping memories that will last a lifetime.

If you are going to have kids, love them.

- Play with them.
- Teach them.
- But don't make them dependent on you forever.
- Teach them independence as early as possible.

Humans used to mature faster. Mozart was a child prodigy and started composing and performing at a remarkably young age. At six years old, in 1762, he traveled with his family to Vienna, where he performed for Empress Maria Theresaat the Schönbrunn Palace. He played the harpsichord for the Empress and her family, including Marie Antoinette (who was also a child at the time). It is said that young Mozart was so confident and charming that he jumped onto Maria Theresa's lap and hugged her.

What happened?

Why are we raising generations of mentally weak, easily distracted, dependent adults?

- Technology.
- Overprotection.
- Lack of real-world exposure.

Children today are not given space to explore, to think for themselves, to solve problems. Their brains are drowned in screens, in constant digital noise, in the passive consumption of endless content.

We are disconnecting from the very things that make us human—from nature, from creativity, from self-reliance.

When a child is born, their brain is still developing. In the beginning, they rely more on instinct than cognitive reasoning. As they grow, it's important not to program out those natural instincts. Give them space to explore, learn, and adapt in their own way. Observe, guide, and course-correct when needed—but don't limit them. And above all, avoid programming fear. Fear restricts growth, creativity, and confidence. A child who is taught to navigate life with curiosity rather than anxiety will develop resilience, adaptability, and a strong sense of self.

Children have their own vision for their lives, their own dreams, even from a very young age. Don't impose your expectations on them—nurture their imagination instead. Encourage them to dream, to explore, to shape their own future.

One simple way to help children develop a positive mindset is by saying: Close your eyes, think about all the good things you want in life, and sleep. Let them learn the power of positive programming early on—teaching them to focus on possibility rather than limitation.

If there's one thing I appreciate most about my mother's parenting, it's exactly this. Being a single mom, she couldn't always create a perfect environment, nor did she have the luxury of shielding me from every hardship. But this—this small, simple ritual—stayed with me. It became an anchor, a quiet act of resilience in the midst of chaos.

This practice, though seemingly small, shaped my approach to life. It became the foundation for how I reset, how I built confidence, how I trained my subconscious to believe in better days—even when the present didn't reflect them.

And that is the power of early programming. A simple thought before sleep can turn into a lifelong mindset.

Humans are born with only two innate fears: the fear of heights and the fear of loud noises. These survival instincts are hardwired into our brains, protecting us from potential dangers. Studies, like the **visual cliff experiment**, show that even infants instinctively avoid perceived drops, while the **Moro reflex** causes newborns to startle at sudden loud sounds. Every other fear—whether of failure, rejection, or the unknown—is learned through experience and conditioning. This means that most of what holds us back in life isn't natural—it's programmed. And what's programmed can be rewritten.

The Turning Point: When Life Reshapes Your Mindset

Loss changes people in ways they may not even realize. When we lost our father, it shaped two distinct mentalities. My sister, at eight years old, understood the permanence of death in a way I couldn't at five. For her, the world suddenly became a place of uncertainty, where the unknown wasn't filled with possibilities but with the looming threat of something going wrong. Fear of loss became her constant companion, subtly influencing her decisions and colouring her perspective.

For me, the impact took a different form. It planted a deep sense of responsibility — a need to protect and care for the people I loved. Even as a child, I acted on that instinct. I remember walking with my mother, instinctively switching sides to shield her from the road. When she asked why, I simply said, *"Just in case a car veers off, I'd rather it hit me than you."* That protective mindset only grew stronger. Years later, when my uncle was diagnosed with multiple sclerosis, I devoted my time to his comfort, spending hours by his side, playing chess or backgammon, and ensuring he never felt alone.

This savior complex followed me into adulthood. I poured myself into the needs of others, often without considering my own. I rarely expected anything in return, but the weight of carrying everyone else's burdens slowly wore me down. Looking back, I realize my actions were fueled by both love and fear — the fear of losing someone else, of facing the helplessness I felt as a child. It's a burden I'm still learning to release.

The truth is, this kind of internal shift can happen at any age. You could be at the peak of success — your career flourishing, your personal life stable — when doubt creeps in. Suddenly, you fear failure. Maybe it's all too good to last. Or perhaps something beyond your control happens, something that cracks the foundation of your confidence. In its wake, fear seeps in, reshaping your mindset into one of caution, hesitation, and quiet anxiety.

When that shift occurs, no amount of self-reassurance — *"I deserve better," "I'll make it," "Everything will be okay"*— can fully erase the fear that the next disaster is just around the corner. That's when you face a choice. You can let fear dictate your actions, allowing it to write the story of your life. Or you can recognize that while loss and setbacks are inevitable, they do not have to define your future. Just as the mind was reshaped by trauma, it can be reprogrammed for resilience.

This works both ways. Positive experiences can wire your mind for success. When life repeatedly affirms that things will work out, it builds confidence. When opportunities lead to growth and challenges are overcome, belief in yourself becomes second nature. Confidence isn't just a trait — it's often the result of consistent reinforcement. The mind learns what it's taught, and with intention, it can be taught to see possibilities instead of obstacles.

Here's the thing — when something shakes you like that, you have to trace it back to its origin. Whether it was a moment of joy or a painful experience, finding the trigger point is essential. Only then can you decide how to move forward.

If it was someone else who caused the harm, you may need to forgive them — not for their sake, but for your own peace, and if the fault was yours, learning to forgive yourself becomes just as crucial. That forgiveness, whether directed outward or inward, is the reset your mind needs. Without it, the pain lingers, dictating your choices and clouding your future.

This is why giving children a safe, loving upbringing is so important. A good childhood builds a foundation of resilience, confidence, and trust. On the other hand, those who carry unresolved pain often spend years in therapy, untangling the roots of their setbacks just to find that origin point. Reprogramming a mind for happiness is possible, but it takes time — and far too many people only begin the process in adulthood.

The truth is, adults should have an advantage. With awareness and intention, they can confront those experiences head-on, understanding the patterns and breaking free from them. It's not easy, but once you face the past, you give yourself the chance to rewrite your future.

Sibling Rivalry: Turning Competition into Teamwork

Building Strong Sibling Bonds

Sibling relationships are foundational to a child's emotional development. The way siblings communicate and resolve conflicts shapes lifelong habits, contributing to their stability, growth, and ability to collaborate as adults. When raised as teammates instead of competitors, siblings build a support system that fosters mutual success instead of resentment.

Raise Siblings as a Team, Not Competitors

1. Model Fairness & Avoid Comparisons

Comparing siblings undermines their individuality and breeds insecurity. Instead of statements like "Why can't you be more like your sister?", celebrate each child's strengths. Acknowledge their unique talents without creating a perceived hierarchy.

2. Encourage Collaboration

Assign team-based tasks that foster cooperation. Encourage siblings to pursue shared goals, like saving for a family trip or caring for a pet together. Celebrate mutual support rather than focusing solely on individual accomplishments.

3. Teach Conflict Resolution

Conflicts are inevitable, but they present opportunities for growth. Guide your children to express their emotions calmly, listen to one another, and find solutions together. Developing these skills will benefit their personal and professional relationships.

4. Avoid Labels

Labeling children ("The Smart One" or "The Funny One") limits their growth and fuels resentment. Let your children define themselves and explore their interests without the pressure of maintaining a specific identity.

5. Foster Connection While Encouraging Individuality

Siblings don't need to be alike to have a strong bond. Support their individual interests while maintaining family traditions that build connection, like weekly movie nights or outdoor activities. Remind them that differences in personality and strengths enrich their relationship rather than diminish it.

6. Emphasize Loyalty and Support

Teach your children that siblings are a lifelong support system. When challenges arise, they should uplift each other rather than judge. This mindset creates resilient, empathetic adults who value collaboration over competition.

The Long-Term Benefits

Siblings who grow up supporting one another carry these values into adulthood. They become better partners, friends, and coworkers, equipped with the emotional intelligence to navigate relationships and challenges. A world where people understand collaboration and mutual growth is one with fewer conflicts and deeper connections.

By fostering teamwork and support, you're not just raising siblings — you're nurturing lifelong allies.

Teenagers: A Work in Progress, Not a Finished Product

As parents, we often get impatient with our teenagers' mistakes. We wonder—How can they not see the consequences? Why do they keep making the same errors? By this point, we see them as mature enough to read, hear, and understand, but we forget one crucial thing: while they may have mastered basic life skills like walking, talking, and reading, they have not yet programmed their brains for many of life's more complex responsibilities.

Think of it this way—learning how to manage time, control impulses, and prioritize responsibilities is just as much a programming process as learning to read or ride a bike. The difference is, we often assume they should already know these things when, in reality, they're still figuring it out.

Take common teenage struggles:

• Waking up late and missing school – It's not defiance; their internal clock is still developing, and they haven't yet built the habit of structured sleep.
• Spending too much time on their phone – It's not about disrespecting family time; their brain is wired to seek stimulation, and they haven't learned the discipline to self-regulate.
• Avoiding responsibilities – They may not yet fully understand how their choices today impact their future.

This isn't a discipline issue—it's a programming issue. Instead of reacting with frustration, find creative ways to guide them. Just like we taught them how to walk or read, we need to teach them how to manage their time, prioritize, and make responsible choices.

So, what's the solution?

• Find what works for them. Not every teenager responds to the same structure.
• Break tasks into habits. Help them automate the things they resist.
• Teach through action, not just words. They learn more from watching you than from being lectured.
• Be patient. Just because they struggle now doesn't mean they won't figure it out.

Parenting doesn't stop at childhood. Teenagers are still being programmed. Your job is to guide, adjust, and help them install the right habits—before life does it for them in ways they might not like.

Final Thoughts:

Parenting, like life itself, is not about perfection. It's about purpose. Every choice we make — from how we nurture our children to how we nurture ourselves — leaves a lasting imprint. The stories we tell, the lessons we teach, and the fears we pass down all shape the world we are building for the next generation.

Perhaps the most important lesson is this: Just as we can shape the minds and futures of our children, we can also reshape our own. The same principles of programming apply to us. Every day is an opportunity to unlearn what no longer serves us, to rewrite outdated beliefs, and to build a mindset that moves us closer to the life we truly want.

Whether you are raising children or simply raising yourself to a higher standard, remember that the legacy you leave is not measured in material wealth or social status. It is reflected in the strength of your character, the depth of your relationships, and the resilience you instill — both in yourself and in those you guide.

Raise your children to face the world with courage and curiosity, but raise yourself, too. Continue learning, adapting, and reprogramming. Because in doing so, you're not just shaping your own story — you're inspiring the stories of those who come after you.

And that is a legacy worth leaving.

Step 6: The Foundation of Relationships

Build a Small, Strong Circle

Keep It Simple
Value the people in your life. Keep your word. Build meaningful connections. Give without expecting—so that when the time comes, you are also open to receiving.
There's a German saying:
"Allen Leuten recht getan, ist eine Kunst, die niemand kann."
Translated: "To do right by everyone is an art no one can master."

Yet, many waste energy trying to please everyone. The truth? You can't win that game. People will judge you no matter what—so live on your own terms.

Build a Small, Strong Circle

Friendships matter, but not all friendships are equal. A large social circle filled with insincere connections is a waste of time.

Surround yourself with people who:

- **Support you** through wins and losses.
- **Show up when it matters**—not just when it benefits them.
- **Give without expectation.**

Friendship isn't a group chat or a list of followers. A true circle uplifts, not drags down. If someone claps when you struggle but vanishes when you succeed, they were never in your corner to begin with.

Live for Yourself, Not Social Media

Stop doing things just for validation. Stop shaping experiences for likes.

Think about it—how many people travel just to post about it?

They budget thousands, yet plan nothing meaningful. They stay in random places, eat random food, exhaust themselves in the summer heat—all for a few forced photos.

For what?

To chase approval from strangers?

Ask yourself:

Are you returning home fulfilled, with real memories and experiences?

Or are you coming back drained, sunburned, and empty?

If it's the latter, reconsider. A picture isn't worth your energy, well-being, or the structure you've built in your life.

Friendships Are for Support, Not Competition

A real friend:

- Celebrates your success, rather than resents it.
- Offers a helping hand, not just a comment.
- Stands by you, even when there's nothing in it for them.

If your circle thrives on gossip, comparison, or social validation, it's time to step back.

You are a product of your environment. The wrong people will drain you.

The right ones?

They'll **elevate you, challenge you, and help you grow.**

Choose wisely.

Final thoughts: In the end, life is about simplicity and meaningful relationships. Choose to live authentically, nurture genuine connections, and free yourself from the need for external validation. When you surround yourself with the right people and stay true to yourself, fulfillment follows naturally. And **here's a challenge for your next catch-up:** When you meet a friend, steer the conversation away from material things. Instead, explore their emotional world — ask how they've really been feeling. Talk about culture, life values, health, growth. Go deeper than the surface.

You might be surprised where the conversation takes you — and how much more connected you feel.

Step 7: Learning How to Learn

We've touched on manifestation already, but now we're returning to clear up misconceptions and help you understand what truly happens — your thoughts aren't just fleeting ideas; they're part of a connected web of energy. The more organized and structured that energy becomes, the more powerful and aligned your outcomes will be. To achieve this, you have to appreciate your brain, nurture it, and help it grow. That's why true "manifestation" programming goes hand in hand with continuous learning — because a sharp, expanded mind is the strongest foundation for creating your reality.

Manifestation is often misunderstood. People think it's about visualizing your dreams until they magically come true, but manifestation is simply mental programming, and it only works if your brain is wired correctly.

Your conscious mind controls your daily thoughts and decisions. It processes information, solves problems, and reacts to immediate situations, but your subconscious mind is far more powerful—it operates beneath the surface, influencing your habits, emotions, and beliefs. The key to manifestation is ensuring that both minds are aligned.

If your conscious mind is flooded with negative thoughts and distractions, your subconscious will follow. Every complaint, self-doubt, and anxious thought feeds a pattern of resistance. The result? You procrastinate, overthink, and sabotage your own goals.

I use this word very carefully as I think there is no such thing as procrastination It's all mental programming. If you spend hours, days, even weeks feeding your subconscious mind the message that you don't want to do something, guess what? You won't do it. You'll delay it, avoid it, resist it—because you've already programmed your mind to reject it. Procrastination isn't laziness; it's the result of negative mental rehearsal. If you want to shift out of that cycle, you have to intentionally reprogram your mind. Tell yourself you want to do it. Visualize it going well. Get excited about it. Your thoughts train your subconscious, and your subconscious drives your behavior. Change the code, change the outcome.

But when your conscious mind is exposed to healthy stimuli—learning, growth, and purposeful action—it programs your subconscious to work toward a better future. Instead of obsessing over what you want, you focus on becoming the kind of person who achieves it. Your subconscious, free from constant worry, has the space to dream and innovate.

This doesn't mean forcing yourself to be overly positive. It means creating a mental environment that supports growth. Replace limiting beliefs with constructive thoughts:

- "I am capable of solving problems."
- "I can learn something new every day."
- "My efforts bring value to my life."

As you maintain this mindset, your subconscious mind will take over. It will quietly align your actions with your long-term goals, helping you make choices that move you closer to the life you want. The more you nurture this internal alignment, the more natural manifestation becomes.

Let your conscious mind manage the daily tasks, while your subconscious mind focuses on the bigger picture—building the life you truly desire. Success isn't about relentless striving; it's about creating the mental conditions that make achievement inevitable. When you trust your subconscious to work for you, every step forward becomes easier and more fulfilling.

Now that we've optimized the mind, let's focus on optimizing the process of learning. Think of yourself as an operating system.

- Today, you're iOS 18.3.
- Tomorrow, you upgrade to iOS 18.4.
- Then iOS 19, iOS 20…

Small, daily upgrades. No overthinking. No resistance. Just continuous progress. The problem with most people? They overcomplicate learning. They make it feel like a burden instead of an automatic process. The solution? Structure. Simplicity. Autopilot. You don't waste time debating whether to learn. You just do it.

Look at language-learning apps. Some thrive, others fail. The successful ones don't just throw information at you. They build habits. Why? Because the brain needs time to process, absorb, and structure information. A child doesn't wake up one day speaking fluently. It takes a full year before they even say "mama" or "papa." The same principle applies to anything you want to learn. The key? Small, daily habits. No overloading. Consistent exposure.

Your brain, like your body, rejects excess. Eat too much? Your body stores it as useless fat. Consume too much information at once? Your brain forgets most of it. It's not about how much you learn in one sitting. It's about how often you engage with it. This is why cramming doesn't work—but daily exposure does.

Here's a truth most people don't realize: Most millionaires, celebrities, and tech geniuses? They're not extraordinary. They just had the right structure, the right habits, and the right mindset. Not everyone is born into privilege. Not everyone has parents who set them up for success, but everyone has access to the most powerful resource in history—information. The question is: Are you using it?

Learning isn't just about acquiring skills. It's about controlling your mind. It keeps you busy—so you don't waste energy on negativity. It keeps you focused—so you don't drown in distractions. It gives you purpose—so you don't spiral into self-pity. A busy mind is a content mind. Keep learning. Keep growing. Keep upgrading yourself.

For all our technological advancements, we still struggle to explain ancient discoveries: The Antikythera Mechanism, a 2,000-year-old analog computer—centuries ahead of its time. Göbekli Tepe, built 11,000 years ago, predating agriculture, yet engineered with precision. The Great Pyramids, Sacsayhuamán, and the Nazca Lines—monuments beyond what we credit early humans with. We assume we've "evolved." But have we? It's not the human brain that has changed. It's our technology. Our ancestors used raw intellect—solving complex problems without automation, AI, or digital tools to think for them. So the real question isn't: Are we smarter than past civilizations? The real question is: Have we lost something in the process?

Work: Passion, Pride, and Purpose

Whatever you do, do it with passion and take pride in the outcome — not for praise or validation, but because it transforms your experience of life. Approaching work with indifference doesn't just make you replaceable; it makes your own life miserable. Without growth, you stagnate; but when you take ownership of your work — whether leading a company, serving coffee, or building from the ground up — your days become purposeful. Challenges become opportunities. Others will notice your passion, and success will naturally follow.

That doesn't mean every job will spark joy. It means finding ways to connect with your work, grow through it, and engage fully. If you don't, you're simply passing time, numbing the hours until the weekend.

Find what excites you. Build on it.

Most professions are as old as humanity itself — cooking, building, crafting. The difference lies in mastery. In a world of mass production, dedication to excellence sets you apart. You don't need to reinvent the wheel; you just need to become exceptional at what you do.

If you don't like your work, don't stay stuck. Spend time learning, improving, or pivoting. You're not unhappy because you're incapable. You're unhappy because you've convinced yourself you're limited — and that's simply not true.

You can learn. You can evolve. You can do anything.

Final Thoughts

Daily learning leads to transformation. It's not about talent or luck; it's about structure, persistence, and a willingness to grow.

Commit to it. Let your curiosity lead the way. The more you learn, the more you unlock your true potential.

Learning isn't a burden—it's your gateway to freedom.

Step 8: Finance and Money Management

Earlier, we explored how thoughts shape reality and how action determines success. Now, we'll apply those principles to **financial discipline and wealth-building**. Despite studying finance and working in the industry, I struggled with money for years. Why? Because financial success isn't just about knowledge—it's about **habits, mindset, and discipline**.

Society conditions us to **chase the wrong values**, prioritizing consumerism over financial independence and material possessions over true fulfillment. It took me years to realize that **simplicity is the key**—a clean, intentional lifestyle eliminates financial stress and unnecessary spending.

A healthy relationship with money isn't about hoarding or overspending—it's about balance. Money is a tool, not something to fear or obsess over. It should offer security, open doors, and enhance the quality of your life—not cause anxiety or become a symbol of excess.

Too often, people confuse extreme frugality with financial discipline. But true wealth isn't built through constant deprivation. Financial independence doesn't mean pinching every penny—it means designing your finances in a way that supports both stability and joy. When money moves effortlessly through systems you've set up—with clarity, discipline, and purpose—it brings freedom, peace of mind, and the ability to shape your future with confidence.

There was a time I could explain financial principles with ease, even give advice that helped others—but I wasn't living by them myself. Working at a bank and reading all the finance books didn't build my wealth. Because knowing what to do isn't enough. Success—financial or otherwise—comes from doing the right things consistently.

Good financial habits aren't automatic. For some, they're passed down early in life; for others, they must be built intentionally. At 30, I was still figuring it out. I was earning more but not growing wealth—still caught in the chase for what society told me success should look like. And then I stripped everything back and found the real answer: simplicity.

Living simply—with purpose—frees you from the weight of consumerism. It makes space for wealth to build naturally. And the same principle applies across your whole life: simplify your health, your relationships, your goals... and everything starts to align.

That's when things shift. You stop chasing, and start creating.

Find a financial consultant who understands how to build wealth, not just manage it. Make your money work for you through smart, intentional investments. Don't fear long-term strategies or strategic debt—wealth is a slow build, not a quick win.

Protect yourself with proper planning, insurance, and reserves—so you're never caught off guard.

Financial success is not about sacrifice—it's about design. What's the point of having money if you never enjoy it? True wealth is about building a life where you have time, choice, freedom… and the ability to share that with people who matter.

The most successful people rarely chase money. They master their craft, pour themselves into something meaningful, and let the money follow. They automate what they can so their energy stays focused on passion, purpose, and excellence. Wealth becomes the result—not the aim.

Every truly wealthy person I've met got there by doing what they love. Whether in art, business, tech, or finance—they didn't pursue money, they pursued mastery. And when you're fully engaged in something that lights you up, money has no choice but to follow.

But the real measure of success isn't what's in your bank account—it's how rich your life feels. If you trade joy, creativity, or love in exchange for money, you'll wake up one day with everything you thought you wanted… and still feel empty.

The key is structure. Build smart systems. Invest wisely. Automate what drains you. Then, allow yourself to live. Buy what adds genuine value, take that trip, invest in your passions, and create memories. Money is never the goal—it's the fuel. The real goal is to build a life you don't need to escape from. One where work and purpose align, where you wake up excited, and where freedom isn't something you long for—it's something you already live.

Not everything should run on autopilot—but anything that feels like a chore should. Automate the dull, repetitive parts of life so you can focus on what truly matters: love, growth, creation, connection.

Managing your money should be efficient and almost invisible—not something that constantly weighs on your mind. When your finances flow with intention in the background, you gain clarity in every other area of your life. The real key to wealth isn't just what you earn—it's how effortlessly your money moves through your life.

But before any of that—before automation, before investment, before growth—you must build the right relationship with money. Everything starts there.

Your mindset around money shapes everything. If you don't have a strong financial foundation, you will never be able to keep the money you earn.
I was never materialistic and my idealistic views of life growing up worked against me.
I'd often find myself setting aside my own wants to prioritize the happiness or comfort of someone I love. Even when what I wanted could have genuinely improved my well-being or productivity, I'd willingly let it go if it meant I could bring a smile to someone else's face.
The truth is, you don't make money by constantly thinking about money.
Just like everything else in life, automate what you can and focus only on the task at hand.

How to Put Your Finances on Autopilot

- **Set Up Automatic Bill Payments** – No more **late fees, missed payments, or stress.** Automate your rent, utilities, and credit card payments.
- **Automate Deposits into Savings & Investments** – The secret to wealth isn't how much you save, but how consistently you save. Even $50 a month compounds over time.
- **Use Automatic Withdrawals for Financial Goals** – Want to save for a **home, emergency fund, or investments?** Set up separate auto-transfers—so you don't have to think about it.
- **Reduce Unnecessary Expenses** – Take one hour **every year** to review your statements and **cancel anything that isn't serving you.**
- **Program Your Subconscious for Financial Discipline** – Just as your mind naturally tracks birthdays, anniversaries, and vacations, train your brain to instinctively track your **financial habits.**

Why automation is the key to financial freedom becomes clear the moment life throws you a curveball.

Unexpected expenses will always come up: **Something breaks and needs to be replaced. A sudden medical bill appears. If you have kids, pets, or dependents, financial surprises are inevitable, but the more you automate, the less stress you have around money.**

Instead of constantly worrying about what's accumulating in your accounts, your focus should be on:

- Increasing your income
- Improving yourself
- Levelling up your skills

The Hidden Connection Between Financial Success & Life Discipline

There's a reason we're discussing money toward the end of this book:

You can't master wealth until you master yourself.

If you're disciplined in every other area of life, your finances will follow.

Money isn't just numbers—it's a reflection of your habits, mindset, and priorities.

When your life is structured, your money will be structured.

Set up the right financial systems, and you'll never have to worry about money again—because it will be working for you in the background.

- Automation leads to freedom.
- Freedom leads to abundance.
- And abundance starts with discipline and structure.

Money & Humanity

Once again, I'll draw a parallel between humans and computers, but that doesn't mean I lose sight of what makes us inherently human.

Your life should be built on values—love, respect, care, high standards, hard work, and education.

Financial success matters, but being a good human matters more.

You won't take money with you when you die.

Enjoy your wealth. Spoil yourself and your loved ones.

There's a difference between being financially responsible and being cheap at the cost of self-respect. Money is a tool, not an enemy. It should flow, be used wisely, and help you build a fulfilling life. When money is hoarded with a scarcity mindset, it controls you—rather than the other way around.

Yes, you can become financially independent by saving every penny, avoiding travel, and spending only on necessities.

But ask yourself:

You might live **80-90 years.**

Only **40-50** of those years will be truly independent.

Have you noticed how fast time flies?

Is it really worth spending your entire life **chasing unnecessary things or depriving yourself of meaningful experiences?**

Balance is key.

Let your **subconscious mind** build the perfect life for you.

Financial freedom isn't just about money—it's about **peace of mind, purpose, and the ability to live on your own terms.**

Discipline, Culture, and the Programming of Success

This book will resonate with people who struggle with discipline—those who never had structure embedded in them from an early age, but for some cultures, discipline comes naturally.

The reality is, in certain cultures, discipline is instilled from childhood. In some families, children are programmed for success. In others, they are left to figure it out on their own.

And let's be honest: **if more parents truly knew what they were doing, society would be a fulfilling place.** A place where people socialize with joy, share experiences openly, and learn from one another without fear. Instead, we live in a world of **backstabbing, self-serving, arrogant, competitive individuals,** all striving for their own gains at the cost of others.

Why?

Because we are slowly **programming out our humanity.**

It's ironic, isn't it? That I'm comparing humans to robots **in order to help you become a better human.** But the truth is, some aspects of life **should** be approached with robotic precision, while others **must** be protected with deep, unwavering values. **Understand where discipline and automation serve you, but never sacrifice kindness, respect, or the ability to extend a helping hand.**

Because at the end of the day, **wealth, power, and status mean nothing if we lose our humanity in the process.**

The goal isn't just personal success. It's about **building a healthier society**—one where discipline, integrity, and human connection **coexist** rather than conflict.

Step 9: Aging with Confidence & Strength

Aging is an inevitable part of life. Yet, with advancements in **science, health, and technology**, we are **aging slower** and living **longer, healthier lives** than ever before. However, society often places **fear around aging**, pushing people into an endless cycle of **chasing youth** through cosmetic procedures, surgeries, and anti-aging products.

There's **nothing wrong** with wanting to look good, trying a new cream, or exploring aesthetic procedures—**as long as you don't fall into the trap** of constantly searching for the *perfect* product or *the* ultimate solution.

I speak from experience. For years, I was a **VIP at cosmetics store**, visiting **cosmetic clinics**, trying every **doctor-recommended treatment** and following **every suggestion** that promised youthful skin. I believed that **the next product** would be *the* thing that kept me looking young.

Then, I did something different.
I **slowed down** and truly **evaluated what actually made me feel good and look good.** And more importantly, I **redefined** what kind of older person I wanted to be.

The First Rule: Stop Thinking About Aging

Aging is only a limitation if you make it one.

- **Don't make excuses.** If you loved to dance, run, or explore in your 20s and 30s, don't stop just because society tells you you're "too old" for it.
- **Refuse to label yourself as "old."** Your body listens to the messages you feed it—don't let negative self-perception slow you down.
- **Ignore society's expectations.** People will remind you of your age enough already. The best way to stay young is to **keep living the way you always have**—with passion and purpose.
- Aging **gracefully** does not mean **denying** that you're aging. It means **owning it** and making the most of it.

The Second Rule: Don't Chase Youth—Chase Strength

Aging doesn't mean you have to **dress like a teenager** or try to fit into the **same clothes from your 20s.**

However, it also doesn't mean you should **give up on your appearance.**

- **Dress clean, stylish, and appropriate** for your stage of life
- **Avoid falling into the "old person" wardrobe.** Wear clothes that fit well, make you feel strong, and **represent your personality.**
- **Take care of your posture.** Nothing ages a person faster than a hunched back and sluggish movement.

Think about it—**what makes people look old?** It's not just wrinkles. It's **how they carry themselves.**

- They stop caring about their appearance.
- They stop learning, growing, and working on themselves.
- They stop walking with confidence.

On the other hand, sometimes you see an **older man or woman who looks incredible**—not because they look "young," but because they look **sharp, strong, and confident.** They aren't tired from working on themselves. **They are still growing**—mentally, physically, and emotionally. They walk with **purpose**, they are **fit,** and they **think sharp.** They have a **confidence that can't be faked or bought**—it comes from a lifetime of personal growth.

The Third Rule: True Aging Is in the Mind, Not the Body

Some **chase youth relentlessly**—some succeed for a while, but many **end up looking insecure next to younger people.**

You see them:

- Wearing inappropriate outfits that don't suit their age.
- Trying to prove they can still "compete" with younger generations.
- Appearing visibly uncomfortable next to someone younger.

But then, you see others who **own their age** with **grace, confidence, and strength.** They are **dressed well, take care of their body, and look incredible**—not because they are young, but because they are thriving in their current stage of life.

The key to aging well is to:

- Stop focusing on your age. Stay in the moment.
- Never stop working on yourself. Growth doesn't have an expiration date.
- Be true to your life stage. Don't try to be 20 again—be the best version of yourself today.
- Find joy in every moment. Aging should be a celebration, not a burden.

Final Thoughts: The Best Version of Yourself at Every Age

Aging is **not a decline**—it's an **evolution.**
The goal isn't to fight against time; the goal is to **make time work for you.**
If you are **constantly improving, learning, and growing**, you will never "feel old."
If you take care of yourself **physically and mentally**, you will always look and feel your best.
If you embrace **every stage of life with confidence**, you will never fear aging.
Aging is **not about staying young—it's about staying powerful.**

Aging is often seen as a process of decline, but in reality, it's a journey toward wisdom. With every passing year, we gather experiences, lessons, and a deeper understanding of life. The challenge isn't growing older—it's making sure we grow **wiser** along the way.

However, wisdom isn't something we invent with age; it's something we inherit. Long before modern science, our ancestors captured life's greatest truths in simple expressions, passed down through generations. These words—rooted in experience, hardship, and deep observation—hold more insight than entire textbooks.

Ancient wisdom has survived because it speaks to something timeless within us. The same struggles, desires, and fears that shaped civilizations thousands of years ago still define us today. By revisiting these words, we don't just learn about history—we learn about **ourselves**

Ancient Wisdom & Cultural Lessons for a Well-Programmed Life

Throughout history, different cultures, religions, and traditions have passed down wisdom through **expressions, idioms, and proverbs**. These short, often poetic phrases contain **centuries of accumulated human experience**—lessons on life, love, relationships, and success. Whether or not you follow a particular faith or belong to a specific culture, **there is universal wisdom hidden in these words** that can help you program your life for better clarity, discipline, and fulfillment.

Lessons on Love & Marriage

Many cultures offer profound wisdom on what it means to build a strong relationship. One of the best expressions I've come across is from **Armenian culture**:

" *մեկ բարձի վրա ծերանաք* "—" May you grow old, resting your heads upon the same pillow.."

This is **the ultimate wish** for newlyweds because **when do two people truly share one pillow?** Not when they are distant, resentful, or disconnected…

Lessons on Patience & Discipline

Many books talk about the importance of **patience and perseverance**, but ancient wisdom captured it long before modern psychology.

"Slow and steady wins the race." (Western)

"A journey of a thousand miles begins with a single step." (Chinese)

"If you want shade, plant a tree today." (African)

All of these share the same message: **nothing worthwhile happens overnight.** Whether you're trying to **build wealth, find love, or master a skill, small daily actions** matter more than sudden bursts of effort.

Practical application: Instead of **rushing toward a goal**, think of your efforts like **planting seeds**. Some will grow in weeks, others in years—but if you plant consistently, you'll always have something flourishing in your life.

Lessons on Strength & Overcoming Hardship

Life will challenge you. How you respond to hardship defines your character. Different cultures capture this truth in different ways:

"Fall seven times, stand up eight." (Japanese)

"Smooth seas do not make skillful sailors." (African)

What do all these mean? **Resilience is the key to success.** You cannot avoid difficulties, but you can **train your mind to withstand them.**

Practical application: The next time life throws a challenge at you, instead of asking *"Why is this happening to me?"*, ask **"How can this make me stronger?"**.

Lessons on Wealth & Financial Independence

Modern finance books will tell you about **saving, investing, and living below your means,** but cultural wisdom has been reinforcing these ideas for centuries.

"A fool and his money are soon parted." (English)

 "Wealth that comes quickly, disappears quickly." (Hebrew)

Practical application: True financial stability is built through **discipline, patience, and smart decisions**—not chasing quick riches.

Lessons on Choosing the Right People in Your Life

"Tell me who your friends are, and I will tell you who you are." (Spanish)

"Lie down with dogs, wake up with fleas." (English)

"If you sit with wise men, you will become wise. If you sit with fools, you will become one." (Middle Eastern)

Your environment shapes you. If you surround yourself with toxic, negative, or aimless people, **you will absorb their energy.** If you stay around **ambitious, kind, and wise people,** you will **naturally grow.**

Practical application: Audit your social circle. **Who uplifts you? Who drains you?** Surround yourself with people who inspire **growth, not gossip.**

Final Thoughts: Why This Wisdom Still Matters Today

Ancient wisdom survived for a reason—because it speaks to **universal truths** that still apply today. These lessons have already been tested across generations, cultures, and different ways of life.

- If you want success, **be patient and build step by step.**
- If you want love, **invest in someone who grows with you.**
- If you want a peaceful mind, **choose your relationships wisely.**

These aren't just **old sayings**—they are **powerful tools** that you can use to reprogram your thinking and create the life you truly want.

The Role of Pets in a Healthy, Balanced Life

A pet is not just a companion—it's an essential part of a **structured, fulfilling, and balanced life.** If you can afford one and don't have health restrictions, getting a pet—preferably a dog (apologies to all cat lovers)—can **enhance your well-being in ways you never expected.**

A dog is more than just a cute addition to your home. It is:

A source of **unconditional love** and emotional support.

A **teacher of responsibility**, especially for children.

A **daily reminder of how to care for your body and mind.**

My dog, my precious Louis, has been one of my greatest teachers.

Every time he gets up from a long nap, he stretches. He listens to his body's instincts. He **sleeps when he's tired, hydrates when he's thirsty, and moves when he needs to.** There's a lesson in that—true strength lies in balance, not burnout.

We, as humans, were programmed by nature the same way. But modern life has dulled these instincts. Instead of listening to our bodies, we rely on alarms, caffeine, and endless distractions to push through exhaustion. We've become disconnected from the **natural intelligence that was built into us.**

Centuries ago, we learned everything by **observing nature.** We **understood when to rest, when to move, what to eat, and how to stay balanced.** Our survival depended on being in sync with the world around us.

Then, we lost touch.

We created artificial schedules, ignored our body's signals, and dismissed the simple truths of nature.

Now, we are trying to get back to what was once **effortless and free.** Suddenly, being healthy, active, and following natural rhythms has become an **expensive luxury,** when in reality, it's the most **fundamental and natural way to live.**

In the Bible, it is said that God created Adam in His own image. What if this wasn't meant to be taken literally? What if it was an allegory for something greater—**not just about creation, but about how we are meant to live and learn?**

What if the message all along wasn't just that we were created in God's image, but that the **ultimate guide to life has always been right in front of us?** Nature itself holds every lesson we need—if only we learn to **watch, listen, and align ourselves with it.**

God is not a distant figure in the sky—**God is embedded in everything around us**. The Earth is not just where we live; it is a **living, breathing system of intelligence, perfectly designed, self-sustaining, and constantly evolving**. Just as the **rivers mirror our blood vessels, the mountains resemble our bones, and the soil nourishes like our gut**, the forces of nature **shape not only our physical bodies but also our consciousness**.

One of the most **powerful**, unseen forces at play is the **Earth's magnetic field**—a silent, invisible force that affects everything from **weather patterns to animal migration, and even human thought**. Our **brains operate on electrical impulses**, and just like a compass aligns with the planet's magnetic field, our **emotions, mental clarity, and sense of direction in life** are influenced by forces we cannot see.

You don't need words to understand the connection between your body and the Earth.

It's something you can sense — in the stillness between breaths, in the pause between heartbeats. We often act as though we're separate from nature, as though we exist outside of it. But that's not reality — it's conditioning.

Biologically, chemically, and structurally, we are made of the same elements as the planet: minerals, water, organic matter, and energy.

Life doesn't just exist around us — it moves through us in the same way it moves through ecosystems. What happens beneath our skin mirrors what happens beneath the soil. Our biology follows the same patterns of growth, decay, and renewal.

The environment isn't something "out there." It's something we participate in every day — with every breath, every bite, every movement.

Our aging mirrors the seasons: we emerge, expand, contract, and rest. These cycles are not just poetic — they are hardwired into the way life functions, in both human beings and the Earth.

We are not visitors on this planet. We are expressions of it.

To forget this is to misunderstand who we are.
To live disconnected from nature is to live disconnected from our own design.

When we recognize the relationship — not as a metaphor, but as a reality — we remember something essential:
We have always been part of the same system. The same intelligence. The same source.

The Sun, the Moon, and the Earth Within Us

Your body is a universe. And just like the real universe, balance keeps it alive.
Think about it: Earth is only livable because of the Sun and the Moon.

The Sun is your brain.
It's the source of energy, logic, and direction. It powers everything.
Without it, nothing functions. No vision, no clarity, no growth. The surface of the sun is all we see, much like our conscious mind — bright, visible, and active. It's true power lies within, in the blazing core that fuels its brilliance, just as the subconscious mind drives our thoughts, actions, and emotions, unseen yet immeasurably strong.

The Earth is your gut.
It's where life begins and where it's sustained.
Your gut is your second brain — it processes, reacts, and keeps you alive without asking for attention. It's the core of health, immunity, and instinct.

The Moon is your heart.

It doesn't power or sustain — it *pulls*. It creates tides, rhythms, rest, romance, longing, and reflection.

The heart is what makes life feel *worth* living.

Without the Moon, Earth's axis would shift.

Without the heart, you lose your emotional gravity.

You need all three.

- Too much Sun, and you burn out.
- Too much Earth, and you stagnate.
- Too much Moon, and you drown in emotion.

When these parts of you are in sync — your brain sharp, your gut balanced, your heart full — that's when you thrive. That's when you create, love, build, and rest in perfect harmony. This is not just philosophy — this is the system of life. And it exists within *you*.

Ancient civilizations understood this instinctively. That's why **meditation, prayer, and deep reflection have always been tied to nature.** They weren't just spiritual practices; they were ways to **tune into the frequencies of the world itself.**

This is why **walking barefoot on the earth, touching water, and breathing fresh air reset our mood**—it's not just psychological. **It's magnetic. It's biological. It's energy.** The Earth doesn't just sustain us; **it communicates with us.**

Learning from Nature: Recalibrating Life Like Louis

Nature is constantly **adapting, optimizing, and evolving.**

Animals don't overthink. They don't hesitate or doubt themselves. They **don't analyze "what if" scenarios**—they adjust, reposition, and keep moving forward.

My dog Louis once gave me a **simple but profound lesson** during a game of tug-of-war.

At first, we were both pulling on opposite ends of the rope, engaged in a challenge.

Then, he suddenly let go.

For a split second, I thought I had won—until I watched as he **repositioned his grip, adjusted his stance, and then grabbed the rope again with a much stronger hold.**

He wasn't giving up. He was **recalculating his approach** to win.

Instead of fighting a **losing battle,** he **stepped back, optimized, and came back smarter.**

Another example, look at a tree in the middle of a storm:

If the wind is strong, it **bends—it doesn't resist head-on.**

Its roots **grow deeper in response to harsh conditions**, making it stronger for the future.

Instead of **resisting nature, it works with it** to survive and thrive.

Now, compare this to how humans often handle challenges:

- **We grip too tightly** to things that no longer serve us—jobs, relationships, or habits that drain us.
- **We resist change,** even when it's inevitable, making life harder than it needs to be.
- **We burn ourselves out** by pushing in the wrong direction, instead of recalibrating and finding a better way forward.

But **nature doesn't work this way—and neither should we.**

The next time life throws a challenge at you, ask yourself:

- Am I gripping too tightly to something that isn't working?
- Is there a smarter, more efficient way to handle this?
- Should I step back, reposition, and then try again from a better angle?

Like Louis. Like the trees. Like nature itself—let go, recalibrate, and take the smarter approach.

That's not giving up. That's learning to **win in a way that actually makes sense.**

Step 10: Death & Choice

I cannot end this book without touching on the **one certainty of life: death.** It is a subject most people avoid, yet it remains one of the deepest and most personal aspects of human existence.

There are countless perspectives on **natural death, medically assisted death, and the role of technology in extending life.** Many religious beliefs firmly oppose any form of assisted passing, arguing that life and death should be left in the hands of a higher power.

If we follow that same logic, isn't artificially prolonging life—keeping someone alive through extreme medical intervention when their body is failing—**also** interfering with fate?

Something to think about:

We live in an era of extraordinary advancements. Donor eggs, donor sperm, surrogate mothers—all incredible innovations that allow us to create life in ways once thought impossible. And yet, when it comes to the end of life, we're far more cautious. Assisted dying remains a deeply debated topic, even though—for some—it may offer a more compassionate and dignified path. Why do we celebrate medical progress when it extends life, but fear it when it allows someone to leave with dignity?

If a person's natural course was to pass at 78 or 80, yet **advancements in medicine keep them alive in suffering far beyond their time**, does that not also go against the idea of divine will?

The reality is, **we don't get to choose whether we come into this world or not.** Shouldn't we, at the very least, **have some say in how we leave?**

Maybe the real conversation should not be about whether we should **interfere**, but rather, how we can approach death with **dignity, peace, and respect for an individual's choice.**

I Am Not Gone

Do not stand in tears for me,
I'm not where you believe I'll be.
Don't let sorrow hold you tight—
Live with courage, chase the light.
Let your days be bold and true,
And feel my love live on in you.
Build a life that makes me proud,
Stand up strong, speak dreams out loud.

I walk beside you in the rain,

In joy, in sorrow, love, and pain.

Each time you pause and think of me,

That moment sets my spirit free.

Look in the mirror—see me there,

In every dream, in every care.

Remember laughter, hugs, and light,

I live within your heart each night.

I haven't gone—I'm still so near,

In every memory, every tear.

I only truly fade from view,

If I am ever lost to you.

Anna Izmirian

Final Thoughts and Suggestions

One of the earliest lessons on the importance of rest, reset, and decluttering comes from the Bible—God rested on the seventh day. Why? Because even the greatest work requires pause and restoration.

This isn't just a religious principle; it's a universal truth. Your mind, like any well-functioning system, needs time to reset. Without it, you risk burnout, mental clutter, and diminishing returns on your efforts. Taking intentional breaks—whether through sleep, quiet reflection, or simplifying your life—isn't laziness. It's a necessary part of sustainable success.

No matter how far you go in life, keep one simple rule in mind:

- **Declutter.**
- **Declutter your space** – A clean, organized home fosters a clear, focused mind.
- **Declutter your life** – Reduce unnecessary obligations, toxic relationships, and distractions.
- **Declutter your finances** – Cut excess spending and avoid financial stress.
- **Declutter your responsibilities** – Don't overburden yourself or your children with unnecessary obligations.
- **Declutter your thoughts** – Free your mind from mental clutter, useless information, and external noise.

When you stop **clearing space for yourself**—mentally, physically, emotionally—you get trapped in **greed, overindulgence, and self-destruction.**

We see it happen all the time:

- **Money without meaning** turns into addiction.
- **Success without self-awareness** turns into arrogance.
- **Power without balance** turns into scandal.

How many times have we seen **famous, successful people** self-destruct?

It starts with **ignoring simple truths.**

It starts with **losing sight of what matters.**

Declutter. Reinvent. Restart. Refresh.

- Declutter your life before it starts controlling you.
- Reinvent yourself when you feel stuck.
- Restart when necessary—there is no shame in beginning again.
- Refresh your mind—never stop evolving.

Because without these things, success becomes meaningless.

So before you get lost in chasing more, remind yourself:

Success is not about accumulation—it's about clarity, balance, and being at peace with yourself.

The Power of Rebirth: Allowing Yourself to Start Again

One of the most important things in life is rebirth—the ability to start fresh, to renew yourself, and to let go of what no longer serves you.

In Chinese astrology, I was born under the sign of the Dragon. What makes the Dragon unique is that it's the only mythical creature in the zodiac—a combination of different animals, taking strength from each one. The Dragon is a powerful and revered symbol in Chinese culture, often associated with wisdom, strength, and transformation. But beyond that, what fascinated me the most is that the Dragon is sometimes linked to the Phoenix, the legendary bird that rises from its own ashes, reborn stronger than before.

Now, I won't try to convince you of astrology—some people believe in it religiously, while others dismiss it entirely, but what I can say from personal experience is that, after knowing thousands of people and cross-referencing their personalities with their zodiac traits, I have noticed **patterns**. There are certain traits that seem to align, even across different cultures and belief systems.

But that's not the point.

The real lesson I took from this is the importance of rebirth—not as a mystical idea, but as a **practical and necessary** part of life.

Why Rebirth Matters

Life is full of challenges—**heartbreak, failures, disappointments, loss**. Many people try to push through the pain, to keep moving forward without ever truly **processing their emotions or resetting their minds**. But here's the truth:

You **cannot** build something new on a **foundation of cluttered thoughts, unresolved pain, and emotional baggage**.

Just like a computer that starts glitching when overloaded with unnecessary files, your **mind needs a reboot**. You need to **purge** the emotional weight before you can move forward with clarity and purpose.

Think of it as:

- **Rebooting a system** after a crash.
- **Wiping the slate clean** to start fresh.
- **Returning to factory settings**—not to erase who you are, but to remove everything that's clouding your true self.

This applies to **every major life transition**:

- A **breakup or divorce**—You need time to reset, not just jump into another relationship carrying the same wounds.
- A **career failure**—You need space to reassess, learn, and strategize before chasing the next opportunity.

- The **loss of a loved one**—Grieving is not about "moving on" quickly but about **giving yourself the time to heal** and redefine life without them.

If you don't **wipe the emotional slate clean**, you **risk spiraling**—carrying pain from the past into every future situation, turning bitterness into a permanent state of mind.

How to Allow Rebirth

- **Acknowledge the Pain** – Don't suppress it. Feel it, process it, but don't let it define you.
- **Give Yourself Space** – Take a break from distractions, from social media, from people who cloud your clarity.
- **Declutter Mentally & Emotionally** – Write things down, meditate, go for walks—let your mind filter out what it no longer needs.
- **Find the Lesson** – Every pain, every loss, every failure has something to teach you. Take the lesson, leave the pain.
- **Rebuild with Intention** – Once the emotional clutter is gone, start reshaping your life with clear goals and purpose.
- **Most importantly:** Be patient, loving, and kind to yourself.

Whatever energy you give to the world—**positive, negative, chaotic, or peaceful**—will return to you. Rebirth isn't just about **starting over**. It's about **becoming the best version of yourself**, again and again.

Most people spend their lives chasing happiness, yet the more they accumulate—money, possessions, titles—the further they seem from it. We've been conditioned to believe that success equals fulfillment, but true happiness isn't found in excess;

it's found in clarity, purpose, and mastering the mind. The happiest people aren't those who have the most, but those who need the least.

Matthieu Ricard understood this better than most. Once a brilliant French scientist with a promising career in molecular genetics, he abandoned it all in search of something greater—inner peace. He moved to the Himalayas, dedicating his life to meditation, simplicity, and the pursuit of true happiness. His decision to detach from material wealth and societal expectations led him to a deeper understanding of the mind, earning him the title of "the happiest person in the world" after neuroscientists studied his brain activity during meditation. Unlike fleeting pleasure or the temporary highs of success, Ricard's happiness was cultivated through discipline, mindfulness, and an unwavering focus on compassion. His story is a testament to the idea that fulfillment isn't found in chasing more—it's found in mastering the mind, eliminating unnecessary desires, and aligning life with one's deepest values.

But not everyone is willing to take that journey. **Рожденный ползать летать не может**—"Those born to slither will not fly." My grandfather's favourite expression is a reminder that some people remain stuck in their ways—whether out of fear, complacency, or a refusal to evolve—while others embrace growth and rise beyond their circumstances. Success and self-mastery require transformation, but not everyone is willing to shed their old skin. You must choose: stay grounded in limiting beliefs, or break free and soar.

At the end of the day, life is a **series of choices**, and every choice programs your mind in one direction or another. Whether it's your **health, relationships, finances, or mindset**, everything is built on habits—some conscious, some subconscious. The key is to **take control** of what you allow into your life, **automate the unnecessary**, and **focus your energy on what truly matters**. You are not stuck. You are not powerless. You are simply in need of a recoding — a reinvention, a shift from chaos to clarity, and a rise. The tools are here, the structure is in place, and now it's up to you to **apply them, build your ideal life,** and move forward with clarity, confidence, and purpose.

The Power of What You Feed: Training Your Mind Like a Garden

Whatever you feed the most—whether thoughts, habits, or emotions—is what will grow and take over your life. Your mind is like a garden. If you constantly water the weeds (negative thoughts, fears, bad habits), they will thrive, choking out the space for anything good to flourish. But if you deliberately nourish the right things—health, discipline, love, gratitude, consistency—those are the qualities that will shape your reality.

Think about it:

- **Feed your insecurities**, and they will multiply. The more time you spend dwelling on what's wrong, the more those doubts define you.
- **Feed your anger**, and it will consume you. Holding onto resentment only keeps you trapped in a cycle of negativity.
- **Feed your excuses**, and you'll stay exactly where you are. Every reason why you "can't" do something only reinforces inaction.
- Now, reverse it:
- **Feed discipline**, and it becomes second nature. Small, repeated actions lead to effortless consistency.
- **Feed love and kindness**, and your relationships transform. The more you give, the more you receive.

- **Feed curiosity and learning**, and you will never stop growing. Your mind expands with every new skill, idea, or challenge.

What you choose to nurture will determine the life you build. Starve the distractions, self-doubt, and negativity, and instead, feed the habits, thoughts, and beliefs that move you forward.

No matter how old you get, never neglect the child within you. That inner child is the source of your creativity, curiosity, and joy.

Strength and confidence should come from knowledge, wisdom, and self-awareness, not from manipulating situations or controlling others. The most powerful individuals are not those who scheme or deceive but those who are secure enough in their abilities to navigate life with authenticity and grace.

Feed your mind, expand your understanding, and let personal growth be your foundation. When you approach life with an open mind and a willingness to learn, you evolve naturally—without the need for shortcuts or deception.

Final Commitment: The Life Reset Pledge

Write your own **commitment statement** to yourself.

What are **three things you will start doing differently today?**

How will you **hold yourself accountable?**

The best version of you is waiting—start today.

A Happy Person

A happy person is a content soul,

One who lets their mind stay whole.

Not shaken by doubt, nor lost in the tide,

They walk with confidence, yet know how to rise.

They do not chase, they do not plead,

They do not hunger for praise or need.

For joy is not found in fleeting display,

But in steady growth, in life's quiet ballet.

They feel the change—both body and mind,

Evolving with time, yet never confined.

Alone, they are rich with thoughts to explore,

In company, they give—never keeping a score.

They bring love, patience, wisdom, and grace,

Not for applause, not for a race.

For a happy heart is one that is free,

Living life on its own decree.

Anna Izmirian

Recode Your Life: From Chaos to Clarity: The Workbook

Companion Guide to Mastering Your Life

Every great transformation begins with a single choice: **the decision to stop running outdated scripts.**

No one is coming to save you. No one is going to hand you the perfect life. But everything you need to build it is already within you.

You don't need to be the smartest, richest, or most talented person in the room. You just need to be the one willing to **reprogram your habits, reinvent your mindset, and rise above your old limitations.**

This isn't just a book—it's an operating system for your life.

Now go out and build something extraordinary.

This guide is designed to help you apply the principles from the book into actionable steps. Through exercises, reflections, and guided prompts, you will reinforce your learning and create lasting changes in your life.

Each section corresponds to a chapter from the book and includes:

Reflection Questions – Deep-dive into your thoughts and beliefs.

Action Steps – Small, tangible changes you can implement.

Tracking Sheets – Monitor your progress and results.

How to Use This Workbook Read through each section, complete the exercises, and revisit them periodically to track your transformation. The more you engage, the more effective this process will be.

Step 1: Balance Your Body Before Programming the Mind

Reflection Questions:

What does "balance" mean to you in terms of health?

Are there any signs your body is out of balance (e.g., fatigue, brain fog, digestive issues)?

Have you ever tracked your health markers? If not, what's stopping you?

Action Steps:

1. Schedule a full blood test and review your health markers.

2. Identify one small change in your diet that can improve your energy.

3. Set a sleep goal for the next month and track it.

Progress Tracker:

Date Sleep Hours Energy Levels (1-10) Notes

Step 2: Understanding Your Mind Before Programming It

Reflection Questions:

When was the last time you spent time alone in nature? How did it feel?

What external influences may be shaping your desires?

What do you think you want vs. what you truly want?

Action Steps:

1. Schedule one day for solitude in nature.

2. Write down your top three true desires.

3. Create a morning or nighttime routine for self-reflection.

Exercise: The 5-Whys Technique Pick one of your goals and ask "why" five times to find the deeper motivation behind it.

Step 3: Cleaning Your Space & Refining Your Style

Reflection Questions:

What does your physical space currently say about your mental state?

What's one item you've been holding onto that no longer serves you?

Does your wardrobe reflect the person you want to be?

Action Steps:

1. Declutter one area of your home today.

2. Create a list of 5 wardrobe essentials that align with your personal style.

3. Remove digital clutter from your phone and computer.

Exercise: The 10-Minute Rule Set a timer for 10 minutes and declutter a small space. Repeat daily for a week.

Step 4: Relationships & Finding the Right Partner

Reflection Questions:

What are your non-negotiable values in a relationship?

Do you seek external validation in relationships? Why?

What kind of energy do you bring into your relationships?

Action Steps:

1. Write down three qualities you seek in a partner and ensure you embody them yourself.

2. Practice active listening in your next conversation.

3. Schedule quality time with a loved one without distractions.

Exercise: The Ideal Relationship Vision Write a letter to your future self describing your ideal relationship. Be detailed.

Step 5: Having Kids & Building Families

Reflection Questions:

What are your views on parenting and raising children?

How has technology influenced modern childhood compared to previous generations?

What values do you want to pass down?

Action Steps:

1. Reflect on your own upbringing—what would you keep/change?
2. Define 3 principles you want to teach the next generation.
3. Spend intentional, screen-free time with a child in your life.

Step 6: The Foundation of Relationships

Reflection Questions:

How do you differentiate between true connections and social status-driven relationships?

Do you currently have a small, strong support system? If not, what's missing?

Action Steps:

1. Identify one area of your life where you can simplify.
2. Unfollow three social media accounts that make you feel inadequate.
3. Reach out to a close friend and express gratitude.

Step 7: Learning How to Learn & Overcoming the Illusion of Procrastination

Reflection Questions:

What skills or knowledge do you wish to master?

What's the biggest distraction keeping you from learning?

Do you have a structured system for self-improvement?

Action Steps:

1. Set a goal to learn something new in the next 30 days.
2. Reduce one major distraction in your learning environment.

3. Use the Pomodoro technique to focus on deep work.

Exercise: Mindset Shift Worksheet Identify a 'procrastination habit' that's holding you back and consciously reprogram it with intentional thinking. Visualize the action you need to take, break it down into simple steps, and commit to following through

Step 8: Finance & Money Management

Reflection Questions:

What is your current relationship with money?

Have you ever let consumerism dictate your financial choices?

How do you balance wealth-building with personal fulfillment?

Action Steps:

Track your expenses for the next 30 days.

Set a savings or investment goal.

Identify one unnecessary expense and cut it out.

Exercise: The Wealth Vision Board Create a vision board for your financial future.

Final Thoughts & Next Steps

This workbook is just the beginning. Revisit it often, track your progress, and remember: true transformation comes from consistent action.

Notes and References: "I can't think about that right now. If I do, I'll go crazy. I'll think about that tomorrow." Margaret Mitchell 1936

"Mortal is man, but immortal is his work" Yegishe Charents

"*A relationship is like a road trip. You better pick the right person to be in the car with, or you'll spend the whole journey arguing over directions.*" Unknown source

"

"*Only a fool learns from his own mistakes. The wise man learns from the mistakes of others*" Otto von Bismarck

"*Let's pretend for a second you have that little voice. What does it tell you?*" *The road to Eldorado 2000 animation.*

This book does not constitute an offer or solicitation to buy or sell any financial products, securities, or investments. The strategies and principles discussed are intended to promote general financial literacy, productivity, and personal development.

The author and publisher assume no responsibility for any errors or omissions or for any outcomes resulting from the application of the information provided. By reading this book, you acknowledge that you are solely responsible for your own financial and personal decisions.

Printed in Dunstable, United Kingdom

72593287R00087